"ONE MOMENT, PLEASE...

Mort Crim with a personal observation..."

To millions of his fans, Mort Crim's observations are often inspiration. In over 100 commentaries from his celebrated coast-to-coast radio program this extraordinary reporter uncovers the other side of the news—the unsung heroes, the unmentioned events, the gut issues, human flaws and aspirations—as seen through a highly original perspective. He speaks to all of the people all of the time—on survival, war and peace, black and white, youth and age, government, politics and the courts, the marketplace, religion, life styles and happiness...

In short, here's what's happening, and much, much more. Here are unexpected cameos of everyday life presented with wit, insight, passion and compassion—all available for the first time in print for your continuing pleasure.

ONE MOMENT, PLEASE!

MORT CRIM

PORTAL WARNER PRESS • Anderson, Indiana

To Naomi
with love

ONE MOMENT, PLEASE!

A PORTAL BOOK
Published for Warner Press, Inc., by Pyramid Publications

Paperback edition published May, 1972

ISBN 0-87162-133-9

Library of Congress Catalog Card Number: 71-285284

PORTAL BOOKS are published by Warner Press, Inc.
1200 East 5th Street, Anderson, Indiana 46011, U.S.A.

CONTENTS

FOREWORD

Hidden away in these pages is one little article that tells much about the author of this book. I won't give his secret away. You may feel it on almost every page.

The title, too, is a clue. Perhaps it's also a clue as to why I was tapped to do this. I am, after all, the man who convinced Mort Crim that while he could say anything well, sometimes silence was the best emphasis. I take the honor of having taught him that short phrases, plus silence, say more, and more adequately.

His adaptation of the technique is typical of his total dedication and involvement. He "lives" his work, his family, his community, his world. Here his world is people, or more correctly for Mort, "human beings."

Mini-Commentary is a new slogan for an old idea. They died temporarily as the "names" of radio switched to television. The old commentaries were as hard to write as these. The difference is that these mini-commentaries have to stand alone, and stand the test of time, without the basic support of a related nightly show.

I think you'll find this a charming little book. It is full of one man's values—and he sees many—for a mankind that is so busy rushing beyond the moon. Perhaps mankind needs the refreshing and monumental values of the beautiful, reflective moment—please!

MERRILL MUELLER

PREFACE

Lengthy commentaries are about as welcome at the average radio station these days as Ralph Nader at a meeting of car makers.

The contemporary definition of "lengthy" at the average radio station is: anything over sixty seconds.

Actually, a lot of information can be crammed into sixty seconds, if the writer works at it. Like the creator of a one minute commercial, he must ask himself, "What am I trying to say?", and then, with great economy of words, proceed to say it.

The idea of a mini-commentary, precisely tailored to the realities of modern radio, was a long time in the incubation stage, and was finally put to the test in January of 1971 on WHAS (Louisville, Kentucky) when *One Moment Please* made its on-the-air-debut. It was decided that there would be five one minute commentaries written each week and they would be broadcast six times a day, scattered throughout the broadcast schedule, much the way a commercial sponsor airs his advertising spot campaign. In this way, these mini-commentaries reach, theoretically, six different audiences, their brevity preventing a listener from being offended by repetition—again, like a commercial.

True, it's impossible to say everything about a topic in one minute. But it is possible to say SOMETHING, and that SOMETHING fits into contemporary radio formats. That the time was right for this new concept is evidenced by the fact that radio stations all across the nation are now carrying the One Moment Please series.

Much of my time is now devoted to writing and reporting news for television and some of my friends wonder why I don't give full time to the visual medium. It's because my 19 years as a radio newscaster and reporter convinced me that this medium, sometimes laughingly referred to as "television without pictures," still has fantastic potential, power and purpose.

Radio is immediate. It grabs our attention in the car, the kitchen, or on the beach. Precisely because it has no picture, it stimulates and challenges our imaginations. Radio can make us think. It is a voice and surely no generation was ever in greater need of clear voices to sort out the tangled strands of information and weave them into some meaningful fabric. Radio commentary can focus our thoughts upon an issue, define the issue, and demand of us both emotional and intellectual responses.

So, despite my many years in radio and my recent transition into television, in a very real sense I feel my radio career is just beginning. Reporting the news means involvement with life. It's a dynamic profession, not a static one. It requires a developing sensitivity to people and events. Thus I have reactions to the things I report. *One Moment Please* provides me with the opportunity to go beyond merely reporting the facts about war, race, youth, ecology, government, politics, business, people, etc. It gives me a chance to search out the truth about the facts. John Stuart Mill said it best:

"Very few facts are able to tell their own story without comments to bring out their meaning."

The following pages contain a collection of *One Moment Please* scripts. They've all been broadcast, though not in the order in which they appear. Because of their brevity we have grouped them by topic for continuity and reading ease. If some of the punctuation, or even the phrasing, seems at times unorthodox, remember these scripts were written for the ear rather than the eye.

If the reader detects a basic optimism within these pages, it is intentional, for I am hopeful about man's future. These are not all "happy" essays, for it is the commentator's function to make people think—and act—as well as smile. I do believe in people and in their capacity to face issues and deal with them, if the issues are clearly and honestly presented.

MORT CRIM

"Very few facts are able to tell their own story without comments to bring out their meaning."

JOHN STUART MILL

On Liberty

Some Personal Observations on . . .
PERSPECTIVE

NOW HEAR THIS

It was one of those small, personal experiences which seems to reflect one of the world's big problems. While we were waiting for our food at a carry-out restaurant, the girl behind the counter called off a number, customers glanced at their tickets, but no one moved forward. The girl called out another number . . . then another; still no response. She was frustrated and the customers obviously irritated, as orders stacked up on the counter —unclaimed. Finally, somebody figured out that the numbering system had somehow gone wrong—the customers' checks didn't match the numbers on the orders.

The incident shows what can happen when communications break down—confusion, chaos, anger, and, of course, progress and efficiency come to a screeching halt. There was no production trouble. The food was coming out of the kitchen right on schedule. There was no lack of good intentions. The girl wanted to serve the customers—and they wanted to be served. It was just that the two sides didn't understand each other. They weren't speaking the same language . . . and the system was stopped dead.

CAN DO (HIP! HOORAY! U.S.A.)

When a team is losing, morale suffers. This may explain the national gloom these days; because you and I seem to be losing in the ultimate contests.

We're losing clean water and pure air. We're losing confidence in the quality of our products, the integrity of our institutions, and our technology intimidates us.

Worst of all, we seem to be losing the clear vision and rugged determination which made America the envy of the earth. We aren't sure who the managers or the coaches are. We aren't even sure what positions we're supposed to play. And, if we're young, we may wonder whether we'll get a turn at bat.

Well, the game's not over yet. Ecologists and sociologists may agree that we're trailing badly in the bottom of the ninth; but what's to prevent a rebirth of spirit from turning this game?

Cheering, alone, never won—of course. But it couldn't hurt. We spend so many hours mourning our losses; perhaps it's time, now, to spend a minute or so considering the possibility of winning.

THINK HEALTH

It's always easier to spot a vice than it is to recognize a virtue. We're more apt to point out flaws and defects.

It's the nature of the new business to focus upon society's faults. Indeed, journalists would be derelict in their duty if they failed to direct the public eye toward public problems. Much as the x-ray machine looks for the tumor or the fracture which does not belong in the human body, so the newsman seeks out the abnormality in the body politic.

But diagnosis is only the first step toward cure. It is

14

time, now, for society's other institutions to prescribe solutions and perform the needed social surgery. And without losing our demonstrated ability to recognize America's weaknesses, let's start paying some attention to her strengths.

Not all illness is psychosomatic, but any doctor will tell you a shocking amount of it is. It's doubtful that an individual, or a society, can be much healthier than it *believes* it is.

ALTERNATIVES

There are two kinds of prophets. There's the gloom-and-doom type who sees only disaster ahead; then, there's the prophet who is able to forecast alternatives. He, too, recognizes the dangers. But he knows that proper actions can improve the probable outcome.

Today, unfortunately, those who are writing obituaries seem to outnumber those who are drawing blueprints for the future.

No prophet, worthy of the profession, will deliberately disguise a crisis. Whether he's a clergyman or a commentator, whether he's discussing pollution or revolution, he'll present the problem in all its frightening reality.

But he should remember that human progress is made only when people confront choices. Man still controls his destiny. But man forgets this fact when his leaders fail to remind him.

We are brow-beaten into despair these days by statistics and the answer is not the muzzling of our pessimistic prophets. It is, rather, our insistence that they provide us with alternatives.

RHETORIC OR RESULTS?

When will we ever learn the difference between promise and performance . . . the difference between rhetoric and results?

Great words can blaze a trail for great deeds, to be sure. But words can also get in the way:

UN Secretary General U Thant, after much bitter criticism for his supposed indifference to the plight of Soviet Jews, finally felt compelled to speak out. U Thant revealed that his office had successfully intervened on behalf of 400 Russian Jews trying to flee to Israel. He also acknowledged that his public statement on the matter most certainly would jeopardize his future usefulness in this regard.

Many times, discreet, behind-the-scenes, negotiations are the only effective way to accomplish an objective. This is particularly true where deep emotions and prejudices are involved.

In the early sixties, when my father was working quietly with other community leaders to extend equal rights to black citizens in the southern city where he lived, I suggested doing a national news story about his work. I'll never forget his response: "Son, I don't want publicity. I want results."

EASY ANSWERS

People keep insisting on simple answers. Yet the truth is, today's questions are complex. People want easy solutions, but the problems are difficult and any simple, easy approach probably will fail. This is not a very comforting thought, perhaps, but it is a fact with which we must reckon if we're to find any answers— any solutions—adequate to the challenge of war, crime, pollution, racial harmony, poverty . . . and all the rest.

Often our simple answers have a way of backfiring. A friend of mine—a college professor out in Nebraska—tells a story which illustrates the risk inherent in easy answers. As he relates it, a housewife telephoned the fire department and asked if anyone there knew how to get a skunk out of her basement? The man who answered the phone said, "Sure lady, it's simple. Just spread a trail of bread crumbs from the basement to the back yard." Thirty minutes later the same lady telephoned the same firemen. This time she asked, "Does anyone there know how to get two skunks out of my basement?"

THE ANSWER

Once upon a time we thought education, eventually, would solve our most serious problems. With sufficient knowledge, we thought, men would put away war. Instead, we learned how to articulate our hatred, but not how to eliminate it.

Once upon a time, we thought science—technology—would save us. That dream went up in a mushroom cloud over Hiroshima.

Once upon a time we were told that psychiatry would usher in that long-awaited, better world. But, as British psychiatrist, Doctor Joshua Bierer puts it, "Psychoanalysis . . . promised more than it could fulfill and people have become disillusioned with it."

We must understand the world about us if we're to deal effectively with it. We also need to know ourselves, and psychiatry can significantly increase the dimension of self-awareness. But we should know, by now, that the prosperous and peaceful world of our dreams cannot be attained through knowledge, alone. The answer, ultimately, lies not in our wisdom—but in our will.

17

WITHIN REACH

Our house has a basketball court in the backyard. Ever since we moved there, I had tried to interest my five-year-old son in the game—but with no success. A couple of times he had tried to put the ball through the hoop but his little arms never succeeded in getting it more than half way to the target.

Finally, I decided that what he needed was a basketball hoop low enough that his shots would at least have a chance. It worked. The moment he saw the new backboard being installed just a couple of feet above the top of his head, Albert grabbed the basketball lying nearby and fired it straight at the backboard. His second try rolled around the rim. His third shot swished unerringly through the basket and the look of determination in his eyes told me the little fellow was getting hooked on the game.

That was when a neighbor, who'd helped me install the new backboard said, "You know, even a child has to have *attainable goals*." Perhaps the true test of leadership in this difficult era is the ability to inspire people with attainable goals. My little boy couldn't care less about wasting his time on something he knows can't be done. And I agree.

A POWERFUL WORD

I'm not one of these people who blames all society's ills upon so-called permissiveness. I'm not sure I even know what that term means. However, it does seem to me that all of us could learn to use the word NO better than we do. Most of us have been taught all of our lives, either explicitly or by implication, that yes is good, no is bad. Think positive. Eliminate everything from your life that's negative. And maybe all this emphasis upon the affirmative has turned us into a bunch of yes-men and women.

This came home to me personally some time ago when a friend and colleague suggested that perhaps I was accepting too many invitations to speak at dinners, club meetings, and the like. Pointing out the risks to health, happiness, and family life which are incurred by overextension, this friend said, "Mort, you really need to learn how to say NO."

It's a most useful word, whether we're confronting a *personal* question like how best to invest our time . . . or . . . a *social* decision like how much soot and sewage we're going to let industry pump into our air and water.

There are times when the ability to give a negative answer is a positive virtue.

CLASSROOM ECOLOGY

The Milwaukee Journal reported on an experiment by a first grade teacher. She had noticed that her students, like all normal five- and six-year olds, twisted and turned almost continuously in their straight-backed chairs. So, this teacher provided her class with rocking chairs! Then, instead of squirming through the semester, they spent their days quietly rocking. By the end of the school year, they were at least a full month ahead of their normal reading level. What does that prove? Well, it certainly underscores the importance of the learning-environment in the learning process.

In this ecology-conscious era, when all of us are so up-tight about pollution, maybe it's an appropriate time to consider all aspects of our surroundings and how we relate to them. Garbage, gases, and chemical wastes may be poisoning our land, air, and water. But what about our emotional environment? What effect are noise, clashing color schemes, and visual clutter having

19

upon our emotions? If something as simple as a rocking chair can help a child's learning process, aren't there some simple changes we might make around the office —or home—to increase our usefulness? And, maybe cause us to squirm less?

SORRY ABOUT THAT

I had a couple of ideas for today's commentary. But I didn't have time to develop either of them. I was too busy playing on the back porch. Down on the floor. With some miniature cars . . . and a little guy who'll not be little forever.

I had good intentions. In fact, I was headed for my study, determined to write today's personal observation when he called to me. "Daddy, let's play cars." And I was just about to say, Sorry, son, daddy's got work to do. I was just about to say that, when I remembered— that's what I'd said the last time he wanted to play basketball. And the time he wanted to play hide-and-seek. So I hesitated a moment and that's when he said, "Oh, daddy, I know you won't play cars with me. You've always got work to do."

But that time he was wrong. Because that time, I realized the most important job I have is being a father— So I hope you'll forgive me for this un-fulfilled minute. . . . Somehow, giving him one moment for some personal observation just seemed a little more important—at the time.

Some Personal Observations on . . .
SURVIVAL

OUR SPACESHIP

The astronauts' doctor . . . Dr. Charles Berry . . . was in our city a while back. During a luncheon speech, Doctor Berry discussed that near-fatal Apollo 13 moon-flight. You remember, the spaceship that suffered the oxygen tank explosion—an accident that almost took the lives of three astronauts.

Then Doctor Berry explained how NASA experts on the ground managed to get the crippled spacecraft and its occupants home safely, despite some critical problems in life-support systems.

Apollo 13 made it, because . . . in Doctor Berry's words—"everybody cooperated." The astronauts knew their lives depended upon the judicious use of oxygen and water supplies—upon following the advice radioed up by the ground specialists. Everybody cared. And everybody did his part.

Finally, Dr. Berry flashed up on the screen a full-color slide showing the earth as it appears from space. He reminded us that this little chunk of granite, with its thin covering of air, is a spaceship also. Its crew is growing larger; its problems more critical, its resources in shorter supply. Berry's message was clear: The world can be saved the way Apollo 13 was saved, by caring . . . and cooperating.

NOTHING NEW

What you are about to read comes directly from a report of the United States Commissioner of Patents:

Here it is . . .

"Great and small cities are fouling watercourses and shorelines with their sewage. The logical solution is to recycle the wastes and obtain valuable fertilizer, while at the same time ending menaces to health."

The expert continues . . . "After all, the earth is bountiful, but not inexhaustible. And, we may not continue to violate with impunity this clearly-indicated law."

The report goes on to document with numerous health statistics and chemical analyses the author's pleas for an end to pollution. The report is dated, 1855.

Sounds like it might have come from this morning's newspaper, doesn't it? Yet, people persist in asking, "If the environmental crisis is so bad, why didn't someone tell us about it sooner?" The answer is simple. Someone did. Long before Rachel Carson's SILENT SPRING, scores of experts had warned us. We didn't listen, then. We'd *better* listen, now. A lot of dirty water has gone over the dam since 1855.

TEN MOST WANTED

A person can go to jail in this country for simply assaulting another person. Maim another individual and the penalty is even more severe. Kill the person and the penalty can be life in prison—or even death. Kill more than one person and the murderer is liable to find himself on the FBI's ten most wanted list.

But what about the corporation or corporation executive who assaults not just one person but hundreds—even thousands—with air pollution? What about the white-collared killer whose factory smoke-stacks fill the atmosphere with deadly fumes and toxic vapors . . . substances which wantonly and indiscriminately maim and eventually kill . . . yes, even women and children.

As the evidence continues to mount concerning the unmistakable link between industrial waste and human health, perhaps Ralph Nader's question to a college crowd in Cleveland merits serious consideration. Nader asked: "Why doesn't the government list the nation's TEN MOST-WANTED CORPORATE POLLUTERS?"

LESS IS BETTER

Pick up any newspaper . . . tune in any newscast . . . and you're likely to confront some phase of the environmental crisis; it may be a report about water pollution, a commentary on dirty air, or an account of how our natural resources are being unwisely depleted. Ecologists insist that these are not separate stories at all but, rather, related chapters which tell a single, sorry tale about man's crime against nature.

To be sure, a lot more will be written and spoken before this potentially tragic narrative is finished. But already we are beginning to discern the villain of the piece: his name is consumer. Until recently, he has been the hero of the American drama—the star of the American dream. Bigger and better have been traditionally synonymous in our country. Now, we're learning that *more* is not necessarily good. More people means more consumption, more goods and services. And *that* means —more pollution and more depletion. Such a switch in values has frightening implications. But, to deal with the environmental crisis at any other level is to treat symptoms, not the cause.

SLAYING THE "BIGNESS" MYTH

It's not easy, being part of a generation whose job it is to reverse the thinking of centuries. But that is, precisely, our task—to turn upside down the old, and now obsolete, notion that big always equals better. One of the most sacred tenets of the American creed holds that progress and growth are siamese twins . . . inseparable. If a city grows . . . if a pay-check grows . . . if a business expands . . . that's good. Reductions, of any kind, are bad. At least, we've been conditioned to think so.

Now we learn that the severity of the pollution crisis seems to be in direct proportion to our population growth . . . and . . . our industrial and technological expansion. Reduce population—decrease production—and—ergo—you've diminished the pollution problem. Even businesses are discovering this new truth; witness the bankruptcy of Penn Central . . . and the financial crisis faced by Lockheed.

Actually, we can find very early evidence of the hazards which sometimes accompany bigness. Consider the dinosaur, a prehistoric monster which was simply too big to survive.

STATUS QUO VADIS

Occasionally, something of my old-world heritage seems to rise up and rebel against contemporary culture. For instance, the rule which says never save for tomorrow what can be thrown away today. Call it ancestral German frugality, but I've always preferred repairing to replacing. Such an old-fashioned notion, of course, runs counter to one of industrial society's basic

24

economic assumptions—the principle of *planned obsolescence*. More often than not, my concept of fixing the old instead of buying the new proves unworkable. It's as though industry and labor had conspired to make replacement more economical than repair.

Besides the shoddy workmanship which makes many so-called durable goods not very durable at all, we've deliberately developed entire lines of disposable products—from diapers and dresses to sweeper bags and bathroom cups.

Environmentalists know the throw-away syndrome is bad ecology. Now, some leading economists are beginning to question whether it's really a valid economic principle. Perhaps permanence and prosperity are not incompatible, after all.

GEORGE CAN'T

We hardly need reminding that ours is an age of specialized responsibility. Whatever the problem, there's a special person or agency to handle it. Once upon a time the phrase "Let George do it" symbolized buck-passing between individuals. Now, we pass the buck to agencies . . . the police department . . . the Red Cross . . . school . . . church . . . welfare department . . .

For every need, there seems to be an institutionalized answer: Only, that isn't always true. There are some problems which can only be solved through the combined efforts of individuals and organizations. Take litter, for instance:

True, every city has a sanitation department, responsible for cleaning the streets; and, ordinances prohibiting private property from becoming public eyesores. But laws and *street cleaners alone* can't do the job. One woman I know, who walks a lot, always carries a litter bag, stuffing every scrap of paper into it as she goes.

Imagine . . . a gal who's not going to let "George," or the sanitation department, do it, *alone*.

E FOR EFFORT

From now on, there'll be two tags on a lot of grocery-store items in Cedarburg, Wisconsin: The price tag—and a tag with a big letter E on it. That E stands for environment . . . or, ecology, if you prefer. And any item with an E-tag on it will be an item which the Cedarburg Environment Study Committee has determined will not hurt the environment. In other words, if a particular brand of detergent is known to pollute the water supply, it will be deprived of the E-tag. The idea has a lot of merit because it does *two* things. It makes it easier for the consumer to decide which products are ecologically desirable and makes him more conscious of the environmental crisis. But, it also should encourage manufacturers and processors to produce products which pollute less.

The merchants of Cedarburg, Wisconsin, are to be congratulated for going along with this idea. Putting E-tags on products in Cedarburg may not solve the nation's ecology problem—but the good people of Cedarburg do deserve an E for Effort . . . and, hopefully, Example.

GO PLANT A TREE

Harvard biologist, George Wald, says upper-middle-class Americans are to blame for much of the world's environmental abuses. That's because the United States, with only six percent of the world's population, consumes up to fifty percent of the world's irreplaceable resources. Most of the consuming is done by Americans with comfortable incomes.

Well, Doctor Wald may be pleased to know that many Americans are beginning to recognize their ecological responsibilities. For instance: housewives selecting laundry products which pollute less . . . or, refusing to buy non-returnable, throw-away containers.

From Oregon Congressman Wendell Wyatt comes another suggestion for the ecology-minded American: go plant a tree. Wyatt points out that besides adding beauty and reducing noise in downtown areas, every tree is a small oxygen factory.

Wyatt would like to see trees sprouting all over America's urban centers—even in the middle of concrete parking lots. Let's hope his idea takes root.

FUNERAL FOR AN ELM

Some may have thought it was a joke, that Sunday service at Faith Church in Springfield, Massachusetts. But to those who attended, the service and the eulogy were no laughing matter.

They were paying last respects to a tree—a 150-year-old elm, killed by Dutch Elm disease two weeks before the service. They called it a service of celebration and penitence.

Why a funeral for a tree? Doesn't that bear some resemblance to the childhood practice of saying words over a dead bird, or insisting that some solemn ceremony accompany the burial of a pet dog or cat?

Hardly; this service for a fallen tree was anything but childish. The Reverend Eric Basoom spoke of the mutual dependence of men and trees. That group of people gathered on the lawn of Faith Church was testifying to an ecological truth we all must learn. Perhaps Kenneth Clark said it best: 'We are a part of a great whole, which for convenience we call Nature. All living things are brothers and sisters.'

27

MOTHER (NATURE) KNOWS BEST

British author, John Fowles, says America's ecology crisis is rooted in history. For instance, the early settlers can hardly be blamed for viewing nature as their greatest enemy, robbing them of harvests, health, and sometimes, life itself. Nor can they be faulted for figuring there was plenty more virgin territory just beyond the spot they'd 'spoiled.' There was.

Fowles thinks the negative attitudes fostered in those early years continue to shape our actions. Take the typical, suburban back-yard. It's rather sterile—green and manicured—but with the native plants, the so-called weeds, and pests, poisoned out of existence.

Fowles calls for a change in our whole concept of gardening. He says let nature take its course. Forget the crab-grass, the insects, the pesticides and let Nature take over. Well, without realizing our considerable contribution to conservation, *some of us have been doing that for years.*

DETROIT CAN DO

There was much weeping and gnashing of teeth in Detroit when the federal government issued final standards on auto exhaust pollution. The Environmental Protection Agency ruled that the auto industry must develop cars which produce 90%-less pollution by 1975.

The American geniuses who brought us hidden windshield wipers, five-way adjustable seats, living stereo, and self-adjusting brakes—insisted such standards are *unrealistic,* some said, *impossible.* The fact is, the automobile industry already has—on paper—most of the technology needed to do it. This added pressure from Washington should provide additional impetus for developing the rest of it.

When President Kennedy set a manned-moon-landing as a national goal within ten years, space scientists knew they'd have to develop technology—and materials —which didn't then exist. But I never heard one of them complain, "We can't do it." The handwriting is in the sky, Detroit—the dirty air which chokes our cities is saying, "You must do it."

TALK TO THE ANIMALS

Waiting for evidence to become proof can be a life-or-death matter. So far, there is no *proof* that lead in our polluted air is killing us and, in the process, giving us headaches, pains, slow reflexes, and in general making us lethargic. No proof . . . but quite a lot of evidence. Some of it can be found at the Staten Island New York zoo, where a build-up of lead in some of the animals strongly suggests it.

A team of doctors conducted a study of animal ailments at the zoo: Among other findings, they discovered a sick black panther being treated for the second time to rid his body of lead. Last November his brother was found, dead, his body literally loaded with lead. Again, there's no proof that the lead killed him. High levels of lead also were found in dead snakes and dead mice at the zoo. Some of the lead comes from industrial smokestacks. But a lot of it—in fact, most of it, comes from cars. If we could talk to the animals, they'd probably tell us it's time to get the lead out . . . *of our gas!*

PREVENTION OR CURE?

Dwight Minnich says the best way to avoid pollutants is not to make them in the first place. Gasoline is a major pollutant.

So, Minnich, a former aerospace engineer, has developed an automotive engine which runs on a mixture of hydrogen and oxygen substances about as non-polluting as you can find. And, it works.

Minnich and three engineer-friends of his in Perris, California, have put one of the engines in a pick-up truck. They admit the hydrogen-oxygen fuel system has its dangers. But then, so does gasoline—as anyone knows who's ever witnessed the fiery results of a bad collision. And there are other problems—such as lubrication and cooling. However, they are not insoluable. After all, we've gone to the moon using the hydrogen-oxygen fuel system. Those billions we've spent in space will turn out to be a good investment, indeed, if the same technology can now produce a pollution-free car.

Minnich and his friends spent about $8,000 developing their engine. Surely Detroit—with all its brains and resources can meet the federal government's 1975 clean-air deadline . . . if the car-makers really put their collective hearts into it.

BIG WHEELS

Norman Lezin was looking out over the parking lot at the Santa Cruz, California factory where he's president. He got to thinking how much money all those employees were paying just to park their cars in that lot all day. Besides, driving to and from work simply added pollution to the air, and it didn't do anything for the physical well-being of the workers, either.

So, Lezin came up with an incentive plan. The

30

company would make a small contribution toward the purchase of a bicycle for any employee who wanted one—arrange a favorable deal with a local bike shop—and even provide term-financing.

Lezin expected some response, but he was totally unprepared for the outright enthusiasm his plan generated. Seventy-five workers signed up immediately, and the wives of twenty-five employees joined the bike movement.

The plan has made the workers friendlier with each other, too. Lezin says not only do the bike-enthusiasts find themselves drawn together in conversation—they're even organizing week-end tours.

FIRE WITHOUT WHAT?

Here's an item which should interest every city official who's ever wondered what could be done about dirty incinerator smoke. In some cities the municipally-operated incinerator is a major contributor to air pollution.

Now DuPont has come up with a device which blows a curtain of air across the incinerator fire. Oxygen, of course, makes a fire burn faster and hotter—as any camper knows who's ever blown smoldering embers into flashes of flame.

By forcing highly concentrated air onto the fire, this device makes the fire so hot it burns particles which ordinarily go into the atmosphere as smoke.

The machine is powered by a 40-horsepower motor and can force 16-hundred cubic feet of air per minute onto a fire. In one demonstration test, the device was used out in the open. A pile of dead trees was bulldozed into a pit. When ignited, thick smoke columns rose from the fire . . . until the Air Curtain machine was turned on. Then, almost instantly, the smoke completely disappeared although the trees continued to burn.

Perhaps it'll always be true that where there's smoke there's fire. But maybe now, we *can* have fire without smoke.

POWER TO THE PEOPLE

The private power companies aren't going to like it, (but let's hope Congress does)—the plan, to set up a national power grid—a coast-to-coast, interconnected electrical system—could cut way down on pollution and, at the same time, significantly reduce the danger of power failures.

If you're familiar with the role power-generating plants play in fouling the air you will applaud any reasonable step for reducing power-plant pollution.

And anyone who lived through the massive New York City blackout, as I did, back in 1965, should welcome any practical system designed to avoid a recurrence. Such major power failures are much more than a nuisance—they constitute a serious public danger.

A National grid could draw electrical power from one state to another through a network of power systems. This would mean, for instance, that New York during the peak morning hours could pull power from California, where the citizens wouldn't be out of bed yet. The idea of a national power grid is 20 years old— but now it's become technically feasible. Let's hope this "power-to-the-people" project really turns Washington on.

CRISIS COOPERATION

Pollution respects no boundaries. The same industrial waste which pollutes the lakes and streams in southern Canada, poisons the waters of northern Michigan and Minnesota. And, dirty air is blind to national boundaries. It fouls the atmosphere over East and West Berlin, and no brick, barbed wire, or mine-field can prevent its free passage.

Americans may not yet fully appreciate this aspect of the ecology crisis, but Europeans are beginning to understand that pollution is a world problem. It transcends even ideological rivalries.

The "Economist" of London has urged a "think Europe" approach to protection of the environment. But the same polluted oceans which wash the continent, also bathe the beaches of Asia, Africa, and America.

Hubert Humphrey of Minnesota says the solution lies in an all-out effort by the United Nations.

If ever there was a crisis which should inspire international cooperation the ecology crisis is it. Even Peking and Washington are going to hang together on this one—or they'll hang separately.

A WORSE FATE

Whenever the subject is the population crisis, inevitably, the talk turns to food—and how to produce enough of it. That is, to be sure, a very real part of the population problem in a world where millions continue to die each year from starvation.

But there may be even more compelling reasons for limiting population than the obvious strain unchecked growth would place upon the world's food supplies.

Walter Pawley, director of the World Food and Agricultural Organization, says the big threat comes from the intolerable economic and social conditions which would result. Pollution and poverty, illiteracy and unemployment, and of course, inevitable political conflict.

Pawley says the world might even solve its food problems through irrigation of vast desert areas—once an economical way has been found to de-salt sea water.

But unlimited population growth would doom the poor nations to become even poorer, and the wealthy nations, more difficult to administer. No, if population pressures aren't eased, future generations may find mass starvation among the least of their worries.

CREATIVE COMPETITION

What motivates a man to fly a single-engined airplane across the Atlantic? Or climb Mount Everest? Or try to see how many hours he can sit atop a flag-pole or bounce a basketball or kiss a girl?

Ross McWhirter and his brother, Norris, have put together a book of world records. From their research, the McWhirter brothers have concluded that people who accept these various challenges have at least one thing in common—the *compulsive desire to compete*— a motivation stronger than fame or money.

But the urge is not limited simply to those who try to break records. All of us have it, to some degree. The competitive urge is a human characteristic. And few would argue with the McWhirter brothers' conclusion that it's better to try to *out-do* somebody on the friendly field of competition than to try out-gunning him on the battlefield.

Well, how about contests between cities to clean up air or water pollution? What about an international competition to see who can get rid of his nuclear stock-piles the fastest? In competitions like that, there could be no losers.

Some Personal Observations on . . .
WAR AND PEACE

INTERNATIONAL HARMONY

Wise men have always admitted the folly of fighting. Now, even fools are beginning to recognize the ultimate futility of it. Perhaps violinist Isaac Stern finally has provided us with an alternative to war.

He suggests that musicians ought to be the world's leaders. If we had maestros instead of politicians in Washington, Moscow, and Peking, the whole world would be marching to more peaceful drums.

For instance, if the super powers had a "score" to settle, they would simply mobilize their woodwind regiments, their stringed divisions, and order them into symphonic combat. For the true militarists, there would always be marching band contests, complete with uniforms and banners unfurled. Nations could carry on their police-actions in recital halls around the globe. But their really big, all-out conflicts would be staged on some super battlefield—such as the Hollywood Bowl.

Admittedly, it's a crazy approach to solving international disagreements.

Almost as absurd as war.

IS WAR INEVITABLE? THINK-TANKS
FOR PEACE PUTSCH

Most people figure only two things are inevitable—death and taxes. Actually, we might add a third: war. For most people consider war the permanent condition of the planet—as certain and as constant as death itself. Now, some are beginning to wonder whether such pessimism is justified, or, whether in the nuclear age, such surrender to fatalism can even be tolerated.

After all, we spend money and invest a lot of brainpower in an effort to clean up air pollution, build better bridges, and develop safer, more efficient products. Why not some scientific research into the *problem of war* . . . and, what *causes* it . . . and, how to PREVENT it?

At this very moment, a group of social scientists at the University of Michigan is making just such a study. And, thanks to a $149,000 grant from the National Science Foundation, they'll be able to continue their work for the next several years.

Admittedly, war is a more complex problem than, for instance, building a better mousetrap or a more efficient car. No problem of our time is more deserving of a solution! If we don't solve this one, even a victory over cancer would be—ultimately—meaningless.

PEACE "TALK"

I reflected upon Chico Guzman's earlier observation . . . as my son and I watched the famous dare-devil motorcyclist 'gun' his shiny, chrome-plated cycle across a high-wire with his wife on a trapeze suspended from the big bike. It was dangerous, no question about that. Despite the hundreds of times Chico and Monique had performed this act, there was still nothing between them and instant death, except their raw courage and love of performing.

Just before the circus opened, Chico told a local reporter that American audiences, the adults at least, come to the circus because they love danger. They want it. Some even want blood. Chico said he's heard circus patrons *shout for him to fall from the wire.* He said it doesn't make him mad—just makes him a better showman.

Well, it doesn't make me mad, either. But it does make me sad. It underscores once again what the President's Commission on Violence told us and (what every newsman's experience confirms), that *we Americans are a violent people.* Too often there is peace on our lips—but blood in our eyes.

WHO'S TO BLAME?

Ask any ten people, at random, "Who's to blame for the war in Vietnam," and you'll probably get ten different answers. The Pentagon, the President, the Congress, the military-industrial complex, North Vietnam, the list of scapegoats is endless.

To whatever degree any or all of those named share responsibility for the tragedy that is Vietnam, the fact is, none is *totally* to blame.

Senator Mark Hatfield said it quite well during a peace panel discussion in Boston, recently—"It's easy to blame the military for Vietnam," but he added, "We, as a people, have a grave responsibility for our involvement." Hatfield suggested that we have failed in our role as citizens by accepting war as a way of life.

The next time someone brings up the old question, "Who's to blame for Vietnam," why don't we shock them with an honest answer, for a change, and say, "We are."

NO SWEAT

Shortly after that accidental Civil Defense Alert, warning radio and television stations of a national emergency which didn't exist, some reporters in Miami did a little snooping around the Dade County Civil Defense Office.*

They discovered a series of pre-recorded messages perhaps unique in the nation. Messages prepared for broadcast in case of a real enemy attack. One was labeled RETALIATION TAPE and a voice on it says, "Although the enemy has struck the first blow, our Strategic Air Command and naval units have devastated many of his major cities and industrial centers."

Other tapes offer reassurance that the probability of victory is good or provide safety and survival instructions and urge the citizens to remain calm. One can only guess at the panic these announcements would have caused, had that accidental alert been taken seriously and these tapes broadcast. Besides, if there is a real, honest-to-goodness nuclear attack, who'll be around to hear them?

NEGATIVE TO POSITIVE

Peaceful co-existence, I suppose, is as much as many of us have dared to hope for in this era of international hostility and suspicion. We may not like the idea of living on the edge of the nuclear precipice, protected only by mutual fear of each other. Still, even so fragile a peace seems preferable to an atomic Armageddon.

Maybe there is a higher, loftier, better dream. Perhaps we could step beyond our present balance of terror; Britain's foreign secretary, Sir Alec Douglas-Home,

*Broadcast on March 16, 1971

thinks we can—and should. In a dinner address before the Muscovite Society in London, Sir Alec declared the concept of *"peaceful co-existence" wasteful.* He suggested it be abandoned in favor of a policy of "friendly cooperation."

In other words, why content ourselves with simply avoiding armed conflict? Why not seek *active* cooperation in those areas where we share common concerns —such as protection of the environment? Why not eliminate the negative, and accentuate the positive? Well . . . why not?

FREEDOM IS NOT FREE

Many cold-war terms simply don't apply in this new era of detente, peaceful co-existence, and cooperation. But the validity of Winston Churchill's "iron curtain" phrase was underscored, tragically, during this past independence holiday.*

A story, datelined Eisenstadt, Austria, told how an East German man, his wife, and their three-year-old son, escaped to the west by hiding in the back of a truck —behind the truck's cargo.

As they stopped at a Communist check-point, the little boy began to whimper. His father, frantic with fear that they would be discovered, placed his hand firmly over the child's face.

It was only after the family was safely inside Austria that they noticed the tiny body lying limp in his daddy's arms. The little boy was dead—suffocated by a kind and loving hand that sought only to give the child a chance to grow up, free.

The Communist world has made much progress to-

*Broadcast on July 6, 1971

ward humanizing many of its policies since the scandalous Stalin era. But the iron curtain remains as a constant reminder that *freedom is not free*; and many are still paying for it with their lives.

A GOOD POLICY

Kenya's Ambassador to the United States was in our town, recently, and I asked him to name the most serious problem facing the African continent—today. Ambassador L. O. Kibinge thought for a moment . . . then, he said: "We have many problems . . . the problem of black independence in Rhodesia and South Africa . . . widespread poverty . . . disease . . . many, many problems."

But, he said, you asked what is our *most* serious problem? It is this: "How do we get along with our neighbors?" This, Kibinge insisted, is the historic crisis facing all men in all eras. If we could learn to get along and live and work *together,* he said, then the other problems could be solved.

Many African leaders share the Ambassador's view, so there are regular, informal summit conferences at which the various chiefs-of-state simply sit down in a room and, without agenda, minutes, microphones, and other formalities, ask each other—"Look, what are we fighting about?"

Kibinge says good neighborliness is the cornerstone of Kenya's foreign policy.

And they call Africa . . . the dark continent?

ISOLATION OR REHABILITATION

In an earlier, less-enlightened era, all criminals were presumed to be bad men, morally inferior to the rest of society; punishment and isolation seemed to be their appropriate reward. Then, sociologists and psychologists began to recognize the role that environment plays in the development of the criminal personality. Studies indicated that *some* criminals, at least, are made, not born. Perhaps, then, rehabilitation and understanding were sometimes more appropriate than punishment and removal. Where such enlightened programs have been seriously tried, the results have been encouraging.

Perhaps the day will come when we will recognize that nations—like individuals—may engage in criminal acts because of their history. If punishment and isolation can turn the casual offender into a hardened and dangerous criminal, isn't it just possible our rigid approach toward Communist China might be turning one of the world's delinquents into an incorrigible outlaw? President Nixon's Peking visit may be a small step; but at least it's in the right direction.*

DOES IT AD UP?

International diplomacy is about to don a gray flannel suit. The Nixon Administration is backing a worldwide advertising campaign, to persuade the North Vietnamese to permit international inspection of its POW camps. Madison Avenue is being called upon to bring the pressure of world opinion to bear upon Hanoi. The prospect of this $25,000,000 ad campaign, even if the advertising is being donated, suggests a number of interesting possibilities. For instance, they might want to adapt some current advertising slogans to the campaign:

How about—"We treat our prisoners great! Don't you wish everybody did?"

*Broadcast on February 10, 1971

41

Or—"The International Red Cross—Something to Believe In."

They might borrow the current Pentagon recruitment slogan . . . "The United States Army wants to join you." (On second thought, better forget that one.)

Of course, if all else fails, the ad agency folks might resort to something like: "Warning—Continued secrecy concerning United States war prisoners could be hazardous to your health."

NO BOTTLED ANSWER

Today's young people didn't invent the drug culture. They inherited it. These kids grew up in a pill-popping environment, where every malady comes complete with an easy-to-swallow solution: Aspirin for headaches—Sleeping pills for insomnia—Tranquilizers for slowing down—Pep pills for picking up.

So, against this background of bottled-answers it's hardly surprising that someone finally has come up with the ultimate absurdity in prescriptions: a peace pill . . . a psychological drug to control cruelty. Oh, not that anyone has actually discovered such a drug. But Doctor Kenneth B. Clark thinks science ought to find one. And the suggestion might be funny if it weren't for the fact that Dr. Clark is president of the American Psychological Association.

Dr. Clark believes war, racism, child abuse—practically all cruelty—might be controlled—*if* we just found the right drug.

Perhaps someone should remind Doctor Clark that one of the major crises our society faces today is the result of people trying to find chemical solutions to personal and social problems.

Dr. Clark is black. The American Psychological Association he heads is predominantly white. Just consider what an achievement his preeminence connotes.

Doctor Clark, it's sad to see a man of your stature freaking out on us.

Some Personal Observations on . . .
BLACK AND WHITE

PSYCHOLOGICAL WARFARE

The sexual exploitation of non-white women by white men is as old as United States history itself. The practice began with assaults on Indian maidens, continued through the abuse of slave girls, and exists, even today, in every major city, where white men drive through ghettos looking for black prostitutes.

It's as humiliating to the non-white today as it ever was. And young black men, with their developing sense of self-identity and pride, are especially resentful.

In San Francisco, a group of black youths has declared psychological warfare on white men looking for black women. Their tactics may prove more effective than any legalistic or moralistic approach: these young men have simply armed themselves with notebooks and cameras. Now, any time they see a white man pursuing a prostitute, they jot down his license number and take his picture.

Next step: Trace the license number, get the man's name and address.

Then they send the man's picture—along with an explanation—to his wife, his neighbors, and his employer.

One of the youths says he figures just the sight of somebody taking a picture and jotting down a license number will be enough to really mess up a man's mind.

EVERYBODY OUT OF THE POOL

For years, civil rights advocates had been winning victory after victory in the United States Supreme Court. Then, in a slow but certain shift to the right, the nation's highest court began creating alarm among libertarians, and applause within the ranks of conservatives.

One ruling in Jackson, Mississippi, says cities have a right to close down their public swimming pools, rather than integrate them. But, of course, the court ruling has general application—so now, other cities can, if they wish, order EVERYBODY out of the pool rather than permit everybody in.

The most optimistic liberals claim the decision may not be as bad as it appears, that whites, eventually, will want their pools opened so desperately that they'll give in to integration.

It's a nice theory, but recent history doesn't support it. The real danger is that whites may try to circumvent the spirit of this swimming pool ruling the same way some of them sought to evade school integration—by abandoning public facilities altogether, and creating private ones, quite beyond the long arm of the federal law.

QUALITY, YES; E-QUALITY, NO!!

Busing is back in the news. And, it's got a lot of people up tight . . . The word itself has become such political dynamite that it's rapidly moving to the top of the office-seekers "*no-no*"-list, right next to taxes.

But what's the big deal about busing, anyway? I

mean, we Americans have been *busing* for decades . . . busing rural students to their schools, busing children in outlying sections of city school districts, busing children to church and Sunday School. In fact, the people who manufacture, sell, and operate buses tell us the bus business has never been better in this country.

A federal judge in Indianapolis put his finger on the hypocrisy when he said, "This court regards the outcry made in some quarters against busing as ridiculous in this age of the automobile." He noted that students in school districts adjacent to Indianapolis have been bused for years with never a complaint against the practice.

No, the issue is not transportation, the issue is integration. As the Reverend Glenn Dorris puts it . . . People will bus their children 30 miles for educational quality . . . but not 30 feet for educational E-quality.

HITTING 'EM WHERE IT HURTS

The Michigan Liquor Control Commission has figured out a way to hit racial discrimination where it hurts—right in the old bottle.

So, starting in 1972 . . . liquor licenses will *not* be renewed for any private club in Michigan which discriminates against anyone, because of race, color, or creed.

Private clubs have been one of the most elusive targets for anti-discrimination forces. Usually, state and federal laws have been ineffective in rooting out the discriminatory clauses from the charters of by-laws of private organizations.

This plan has a good chance for success. In effect, the Michigan Liquor Control Commission is saying to the private clubs: Either drop the color bar, or close the beverage bar! It's a good bet most clubs are going to find tee-totaling a tough price to pay for retaining their lily-white complexion.

It may seem a devious way for a state to deal with discrimination. But, who knows? A few more innovations like this one, and the forces for brotherhood and equality might become as proficient as their racist counterparts.

SMASHING THE STEREOTYPES

There was a local election in Los Angeles and one of the issues probably didn't get much national attention, but we think it deserves a second look: The issue: whether to raise the minimum pensions for police and firemen from $250 to $350 a month.

Well, despite heavy opposition, the pension increase was approved—just barely. Responsible for passing it were the voters in predominantly *black* areas of Los Angeles; the heaviest support was in three districts represented by black city councilmen, where the vote was nearly two-to-one in favor, while in the predominantly white San Fernando Valley the measure ran into extremely heavy opposition.

Surprising? We're so susceptible to stereotypes, we just naturally presume middle- and upper-class whites would support their local police, while residents of the ghetto would not. We forget that the ghetto, not the suburb, suffers most from crime—especially crimes of violence. As for the suburbanites who *talk* a lot about law and order—maybe they just weren't quite ready to put their tax money where their bumper stickers were.

WHO BENEFITS?

In most public schools, middle- and upper-middle class children score higher and perform better than youngsters at the lower end of the economic scale. Also, in most public schools, the poorer children tend to be non-whites. These two facts have led some social critics to conclude that black children are intellectually inferior to white children . . . that their learning potential is lower.

Well, the two facts just don't add up that way. It's also a fact that learning potential is related to socio-economic conditions, and youngsters from deprived backgrounds consistently do worse in school than affluent children—whatever their color.

Blaming poor performance on inherent deficiencies is too easy and lets us off the hook. Change the structure of society, so that blacks can break out of their isolation and into the economic mainstream, and you'll change the educational performance of black children; but it will also benefit white kids.

Isolation of any kind is no longer an acceptable policy in this one world of ours. My children need to learn that lesson as much as any black child does: Segregation is a contagious disease, which ravages and distorts the minds of all it infects—regardless of their color.

NEW SOUTH

The phrase "new south" is not just the Atlanta Chamber of Commerce whistling Dixie . . . it's a fact of life. The latest census shows the south gained more in population, education, and economy in the decade of the 60's than any other region. Thirty-one percent of America's people now live in the southern states.

These statistics are enough to make any darn Yankee sit up and take notice. Southern education has made such strides, analysts forecast, it will match the national average by the mid-seventies. Per capita income rose 14% faster in the south than elsewhere, and other indicators verify the quickened pace of economic life in Dixie.

But the most dramatic change has been in race relations. So forcefully have the winds of change been sweeping through the south that one young white man in South Carolina said recently: "I used to be kind of ashamed of my state's bigotry, but we've outgrown all that now."

His progress report may have been premature. But it does give evidence that the south is, indeed, rising again.

A NEW DARK(Y) AGE?

Sometimes it really is the little fox that spoils the grapes. Or, the little insult, that turns sour the sweet progress in race relations.

Take the Kentucky Derby, for instance. Given the black man's long and difficult struggle for dignity and identity in this country, it should not surprise us that most black Americans take offense at being called "darkies." Yet, year after year Stephen Foster's original lyrics about the "darkies being gay" continue to appear in the official program. And right on cue, more than a hundred thousand Derby fans, most of them white, stand and sing those words as one nostalgic voice. "My Old Kentucky Home" may bring tears of Old South pride to the eyes of whites, as newsman Clarence Matthews noted recently, but the song's thoughtless lyrics are more likely to evoke resentment from blacks.

Of course, any suggestion that the offending words be changed is met with emotional resistance, as though tampering with "My Old Kentucky Home" is akin to re-writing the Ten Commandments. Actually, modern man has found even the Scriptures in need of new translations—to make them relevant. Surely it is no more sinful to update Stephen Foster than Saint Paul!

GOING THE SECOND MILE

Most churches these days admit that racial segregation is morally wrong, that it violates both the spirit and the letter of Christianity. Refusing full fellowship to anyone on the basis of skin color can hardly be reconciled with the clear gospel mandates concerning acceptance and brotherhood.

Still, such lip-service has had little noticeable effect when it comes to breaking down the church's own walls of discrimination. The sign out front may proclaim WELCOME—but, few blacks really believe that the word is meant to include them.

Now, in Houston, Texas, a couple of all-white, mostly middle-class congregations, have decided to do *more* than just profess a willingness to accept black members. These two Lutheran churches—Holy Trinity and Lord of Life—have launched an advertising and visitation campaign, aimed at actively recruiting blacks, and other minorities. Even paying lip-service to integration may represent a milestone for white congregations, but these two churches seem determined to go the SECOND mile.

DISCRIMINATION

A lot of people think "discrimination" is a dirty word. And, it is. It means religious or racial prejudice. But the dictionary also defines "discrimination" as 'the ability to make fine distinctions.'

It's been this reporter's experience that there's far too much of the first kind and far too little of the second. Some who denounce discrimination and white supremacy in one breath will endorse black supremacy in the next. And that, too, is discrimination. By what rationale can we condemn violence in Vietnam while condoning it on a college campus?

The solution to America's moral schizophrenia requires both less discrimination—and more. It demands *less* "intolerance of others", but *more* "Capacity for making fine distinctions". It requires the perception to recognize that power—black or white—can corrupt. It means recognizing that killing is barbaric. Whether the victim is a Vietnamese infant—or a cop in the ghetto.

CHILDHOOD IS COLORBLIND

Israel Jones, of Louisville, works at a local, suburban department store.

The other day, Israel was walking down an aisle between two counters, when he heard a little girl call to him.

"Mister, is this your little boy?" she asked?

At first, Jones wasn't sure the child was speaking to him. She appeared to be about four years old. She was holding, by the hand, a small boy two- or three-years old.

Again she called to Mr. Jones, this time looking him straight in the eye.

"Mister, I said is this your little boy? He seems to be lost."

Israel Jones said, "No, young lady, I'm afraid that's not my little boy."

And just about that time, the lost boy's mother came for him. But the brief experience made a lasting impression on Jones. You see, the little lost boy, and the little girl, were both white. Israel Jones is black. He won't soon forget the little girl who had not yet been taught to tell the difference.

Some Personal Observations on . . .
YOUTH AND AGE

LOST GENERATION?

The magazine "Seventeen" has been interviewing young Americans between the ages of fourteen and twenty-two, trying to find out what they *really* think and how they feel about their nation, their society, and their future. The results may be surprising but should be encouraging.

Although 3 out of 4 said there is something basically wrong with American society, nearly 8 out of 10 rejected violence as the only way to correct it.

Two thousand boys and girls responded to the poll—high school and college youngsters. Most described themselves as happy. More than half said they feel somewhat hopeful about America's future. I wonder if a similar survey of adults would produce that much optimism?

On other issues, the majority of young people interviewed agreed that government is not investing enough to combat pollution, poverty, urban problems, and to support education.

The majority oppose legalization of marijuana and 7 out of 10 said they would vote for a qualified woman to be president. Now, a generation of youth with views and attitudes like that, can't be all bad.

IT MAKES SENSE

The supreme courts of at least two states have issued rulings which make the voting rights of college-aged young people complete. The rulings permit college students to register and to vote in their college communities rather than in their home towns. And, without such rulings, the so-called voting "right" of 18 year olds is something of a farce.

Although many college communities are more than a little unhappy about the prospect of youth-domination at the ballot box, the fact is, there's no other logical or fair way to handle the matter. It makes no sense at all for youngsters to vote—by absentee ballot—in their parent's communities when the kids have been out of town and thus, out of touch, with local issues and candidates. On the contrary, most college young people are quite well-informed about political issues and personalities in their campus communities. It's been my observation that they often know more about what's going on than the property-owning natives know.

PATRIOTISM DEFINED

If there's one characteristic of modern youth which offends and even disgusts their elders more than pot, free love, and long hair—it's youth's attitude toward patriotism.

Nothing will light up our newsroom switchboard faster than a televised report showing youngsters burning a flag, tearing up a draft card, or toting a sign which describes the United States in four-letter words.

How come today's kids aren't patriotic? It's a question I hear often as I appear before various civic groups —from women's clubs to lodge meetings and the P.T.A.

Well, there's no doubt about it—attitudes toward patriotism are changing. But does this necessarily mean that today's young Americans have *less* of it than their parents did? Maybe they're trying to tell us that the 'liberty and justice for which it stands' are more important than the *symbol*. Maybe they're trying to say that working to fulfill the American dream is at least equal in importance to flag waving. I don't know—maybe patriotism *has been* rejected by today's kids. Or, is it just possible, they are simply re-defining it?

PAY THEM WITH A SMILE

Every weekday morning, at a certain train station near the Swarthmore College Campus in Philadelphia, you'll see dozens of sleepy-eyed commuters sipping coffee and eating doughnuts. And they've got some Swarthmore students to thank for it.

Like so many student projects, this one began as a war protest. But, today's youngsters seem to have a special sensitivity to dishonesty and anything that smacks of hypocrisy. So, they decided it was wrong, perhaps, to use friendship as a device for selling a point-of-view.

They put away their arguments and their anti-war literature but they kept their coffee urn and continued to buy bags of fresh doughnuts. Now they're out on that platform every morning handing out coffee and doughnuts simply because they've learned how much fun it is to share—with no ulterior motive at all. The kids say so often the concept of sharing does not include the well-educated, the wealthy, or the healthy-elderly in our society. Their little ritual of friendship includes everybody.

Ah, which of these students would have dreamed that

when he finally found his "bag" . . . it'd be filled with doughnuts?

SIGNIFICANT STATISTICS

According to a student poll 17% of America's campus set now consider themselves political radicals. Seven years ago, the figure was only 7%.

And, not all the campuses surveyed were of the eastern-liberal variety. They included Indiana University, the University of South Carolina, Marquette, and Stanford.

The poll also showed increasing unhappiness with the two-party political system. Only 33% were satisfied with the present system. (In the earlier survey, the figure was 58%.)

Perhaps the most dramatic change in attitude, is youth's growing dissatisfaction with the free enterprise system. In the 1963 survey, only about 8% of the students said they favored full socialization of all United States industries. In the most recent poll, the figure is 25%, and nearly half the students now favor socialization of basic industries.

Obviously, something is wrong. Either the capitalistic system hasn't been doing the job or those in charge of it have done a poor job of telling their story. Perhaps it's both.

KIDS CRACK, TOO

People hi-jack airplanes for many reasons—sometimes political—sometimes to escape the law, but sometimes the hi-jacker seems simply to be running from himself. The sad story of Thomas Kelly Marston serves, as well as any, to illustrate the point.

Sixteen years old—a turbulent age for anyone—but

for reasons known only to himself, life was particularly bewildering for Tom Marston. On a morning when he should have gone to school, Tom went, instead, to the airport at his hometown of Mobile, Alabama, boarded a jetliner, and forced the crew, at gunpoint, to fly him to Miami.

Why did he do it? Tom, who had never been in trouble before, told the FBI men who arrested him, he just wanted out of Mobile. He said he was getting bad grades in school and that his parents were on his back.

Fortunately, few adolescents will react to their frustrations the way Thomas did. But his tragic experience should remind all of us of the intense pressures all modern young people are prematurely subjected to these days.

AN ORDINARY KID

If you lived in Garden City, Kansas, you'd probably know the name Diane Jones. Just about everybody in town has seen the twelve-year-old girl astride her quarter horse, Star Dipper, carrying the flag and leading the mounted precision drill team called the Garden City Blue Bells. A lot of the townsfolk have seen Diane compete in the Kansas Western Horsemen's Association contests.

They may not know that she's also a star student—earns mostly A's and B's in her sixth grade class. She sings in the choir, swims a lot in the summer; in fact, there's very little that Diane won't try. Her parents never try to stop her, even though some of her activities may seem risky. After all, that spirited quarter horse has thrown her more than once, breaking her arm one time.

Diane's parents say they've tried awfully hard not to baby Diane, to let her grow up normally and be like anyone else. Well, the record indicates Diane is growing up normally—just like anyone else—despite the fact that Diane Jones has been blind since birth.

THE THIRD "R": REASON

After years of fumbling around trying to discover their proper role where student attire is concerned, many public schools finally have added a fourth R to their curricula—Reason. Now, instead of trying to legislate on the acceptability of each style, most schools are taking a more relaxed attitude toward the whole scene—from slacks and miniskirts, to long hair and mustaches.

For one thing, they've found out it's impractical to try to impose controls in the classroom which mom and dad can't even enforce at home. For another thing, the schools have finally realized that their main job is, after all, to educate, not to decree style.

An Associated Press survey of schools across the country indicates most are now giving up the so-called dress-codes in favor of general policy statements, such as simply requiring the youngsters to comply with health regulations and that their attire not be disruptive. That probably means shoes are a must; and see-through blouses are out! Long hair is fine, as long as it's clean. As for beards, one Seattle student says that's not much of a problem in high school—most guys can't grow them, anyway.

A SOUR VICTORY

For three months, Candy Cooley, of San Diego, and Linda Dankman, of Sacramento, carried on a dating experiment to find out whether young men enjoy being pursued by young women. A part of their sociology studies at the University of California, it involved a complete reversal of the usual sex-roles. For instance, the girls would ask the guys for dates, offer to pick the guys up at their place, insist on opening doors for the boys, paying for their dinners, and even putting their arms around the guys during a drive-in movie.

The men were never told that all this female aggressive behavior was strictly a put-on, in the interest of serious research. They took the whole thing seriously. They would act nervous and embarrassed when the girls would open a door for them. They'd refuse to eat when they learned the girls intended to buy. They'd scrunch up in the seat and act shy when the girls put an arm around them at the movie. After about a dozen such dates, Candy and Linda had enough material to write their paper. They both got an A . . . but neither of them got any telephone calls from the fellows they'd dated.

RENT-A-KID

Any affluent homeowner who's tried to hire someone to cut his lawn, wash his windows, or rake his leaves, knows how tough it is to find such help these days. It's ironic, perhaps, that as the rising incomes in the United States have provided more people with enough money to hire help for burdensome chores, such help has steadily dwindled. The situation is not altogether bad because it indicates that a lot of unskilled adults, who would have been forced to take such menial jobs in earlier years, have now found more meaningful and productive work.

But where does that leave the busy executive or professional man who has money to pay for jobs he simply hasn't time to do himself? Well, take heart, Rent-A-Kid is rushing to the rescue. This federally-financed program of summer employment for low-income high

59

school students hopes to establish Rent-A-Kid offices in nearly all the fifty states. So, in the near future, the well-off homeowner should be able to buy the service he's more than willing to pay for, and, at the same time help some not-so-well-off youngsters who are more than willing to work.

TROUBLEMAKERS MAKE GOOD

Woodbourne Junior High is right at the edge of Baltimore's inner-city. There's been a lot of trouble at Woodbourne—fistfights, petty theft, but that's changing now.

It started when police officers John Pugh and Bill Morrow adopted the policy, "If you can't beat 'em, join 'em." Now, the officers are recruiting trouble-makers to help keep the peace. I should say "ex-trouble makers", because signing these kids up as junior policemen has made a dramatic difference in their actions and their attitudes.

The procedure is simple. One of the officers calls a known trouble-maker aside, counsels him individually about the need to keep things cool and then solicits his help. The result? Vandalism has been cut in half, fighting significantly reduced, and the drug problem practically eliminated.

How have these two policemen succeeded when so many have failed? Perhaps because they don't preach, they don't bully, and they don't take themselves too seriously. For instance, that gift on officer Pugh's desk from students in the school's metal shop—that little, blue *pig*.

LEARNING A LOT

A lot of money, time, and talent are being invested in the wars on killer-diseases such as cancer and heart disease. But there's one condition which has reached epidemic proportions in this country and it's receiving far too little attention. This malady can strike anyone, at any age, but it hits the elderly with greater frequency and greater devastation. It's called loneliness.

There's no Loneliness Fund to finance programs for the forgotten. There's no American Loneliness Society to research and treat this joy-killer, but fortunately, it does not require expert treatment. It responds well to the sincere efforts of non-professionals—provided they *care* . . . like the twenty-six third graders in San Antonio, Texas. They've taken up writing to lonely elderly people as a class project. The youngsters got the idea after reading a newspaper story about the number of telephone calls policemen receive, regularly, from people who are simply lonely. And you can be sure that the twenty-six third graders in San Antonio are learning much more than good penmanship.

LIFE BEGINS AT 76

The next time you hear some 25- or 30-year-old complaining about his failures, tell him about Caroline Cooper. Anyone who feels washed up and done in before they've even reached middle age should be inspired by this 81-year-young co-ed from Fresno, California.

Mrs. Cooper's husband died in 1966. Her children were all grown and living in other parts of the country. Mrs. Cooper could have just turned into a human vegetable . . . but she wasn't about to let that happen; no, sir!

She'd always wanted to go to college; but, with the family to raise, too many things interfered. Finally, with no reason to put off any longer getting the education she'd always dreamed about, Mrs. Cooper enrolled at Fresno City College. She paid her tuition out of social security and old age pension benefits, and got herself a wheelchair for getting around the large campus more easily.

Caroline Cooper hopes to receive her four-year degree next spring. And what will she do after graduation? She says . . . she's going to earn a master's degree.

FOUNTAIN OF YOUTH

It took a long time for people to learn that alcoholism is a disease; one which can be diagnosed, treated, and, in a practical sense, cured. Now, we're beginning to learn that old age, too, is, in a sense, a disease. It's not an inevitable and hopelessly unproductive condition. It is a process which, like other "diseases," can be diagnosed, treated, and, perhaps in time, prevented.

This is not to suggest that the productive life-time of all people can be extended, Methuselah-like, into centuries. But there is a growing body of scientific and medical evidence which strongly suggests the aging process can be delayed and diminished, so that it need not rob the final years of pleasure and usefulness.

Kentucky's former U.S. Representative, John Y. Brown, himself a spry 71, has set up a foundation to study the aging process. Science already has succeeded in adding more years to our lives, so, Brown thinks this is an appropriate time for seeking ways to add more *life* to those years.

Some Personal Observations on . . .
GOVERNMENT,
POLITICS,
and THE COURTS

REPETITION CHEAPENS

Signing a bill into law must be one of the toughest, and most frustrating, jobs a President has to perform. I mean it's not just a simple matter of writing his name on the bottom, the way you and I would sign a check. A ceremonial bill signing may involve several dozen Presidential pens . . . the President, making a short stroke with each, so that various Congressmen and their friends can claim *they* have 'the pen that signed the measure into law.'

A similarly silly process goes on, every day, at the United States Capitol building where workmen run American flags up the pole—and down again—each flag fluttering for only a few seconds. But, this permits untold thousands of Americans to own flags which, technically speaking, 'once flew above the Capitol.'

On one July 4th alone, more than five thousand flags got the run-it-up-the-pole treatment.

Somehow, such charades seem to cheapen the very articles they're meant to hallow. Reminds me of the mimeographed form letter sent to one college freshman

class. It began . . . "To Whom It May Concern: This
college values you as an individual . . ."

SORTING OUT PREJUDICES

Boston Congressman Robert F. Drinan is the only
Roman Catholic priest currently serving in the United
State House. Ordinarily, the House is considered an ex-
cellent spawning ground for would-be Senators. However, Congressman Drinan says he's decided against opposing incumbent Senator Edward Brooke next year.
Brooke is completing his first term in the Senate. He is
sure to run for re-election.

Why won't Drinan run against Brooke? Well, Drinan
is a Democrat, white, and Catholic; Brooke is a Republican, black, and Protestant.

As Drinan explained it to a local newsman in Boston
the other day, it just wouldn't be fair, putting the voters
through that kind of an agonizing choice. Think how
difficult it would be for a voter to sort out his prejudices? What if he liked Democrats, but didn't like Cath-
olics? Or liked blacks even less, but maybe disliked
Protestants even more than Republicans?

Or, what if the voter was a strong Republican but devoted Catholic, or a dedicated Democrat but militant
black? Could be enough to drive a computer crazy. But,
Congressman Drinan, before you make your decision
final, think about this. Maybe if voters had to choose
between a black Republican and a Jesuit Democrat,
they'de be forced to vote issues, not their prejudices.

IT'S IN THE BOOK

America's book-shelves must be straining under the
weight of how-to-do-it volumes. And so far, no effective method has been found for controlling this literary

population-explosion. The Grand Old Party has given birth to one of the newest arrivals—a handy guide for Republican orators, forced to face hostile audiences on campus!

The Republican leadership recognizes that the party's future depends upon its ability to capture the imaginations, and the votes, of the growing youth constituency. So, they've put together this four-page suggestion booklet, complete with a glossary of campus lingo. After all, communication demands that speaker and listener at least understand the same language.

Reduced to its simplest recommendations, the handbook urges avoiding partisan tirades, looking students directly in the eye, keeping cool, and advises, when things get tough, interjecting humor. No doubt the next step is for the campus set to publish a booklet on "how to deal with speakers armed with how-to-do-it books."

DON'T JUST SAY SOMETHING—STAND THERE

One of the most successful fund-raising dinners staged so far this year was the one put on by the Democratic National Committee in Washington.

It had all the usual trappings—a 16-piece orchestra —banquet tables loaded with crab bisque, watercress-salad, French wine—the works. It had a star-studded guest list which, in this case, included all the party's presidential hopefuls, Humphrey, Muskie, Kennedy, McGovern, and the dark-horse candidates as well.

Yes, it was a *typical* fund-raising dinner, except for one minor detail. There were no speeches, in fact, there wasn't even a head table. The politicians fanned out amongst the people, talking, joking, dancing (probably doing a little political horse-trading), but not a single formal speech from any of them. Well, party officials had promised all along that the candidates would be speechless. And the idea proved so overwhelmingly successful, the Democrats raised a million dollars at that dinner.

Should a trend develop, public speakers might have to establish a double-rate card; one price for delivering an address, another for keeping quiet.

HATS OFF TO THE GEORGIA GOVERNOR

Lester Maddox was something less than a hero to Liberals and Civil Rights activists during his tenure as Georgia governor. But Maddox did do one thing even his ideological enemies could applaud, and his successor, Jimmy Carter, is continuing the practice.

Maddox opened his office doors to anyone and everyone who had a problem. They were invited to 'come on in and talk it over with the governor'; whether Democrat or Republican, young or old, white or black. And come in they did, with an assortment of gripes and suggestions as varied as the Georgians themselves.

Governor Carter's style is different. Maddox used to laugh and joke and sympathize with his callers, in loud tones. Carter is quieter. He leads his visitors to a corner of his office, away from newsmen, and discusses their problems in confidence. The style isn't important. What is important is the fact that Carter is carrying on the often neglected duty of all political leaders: *the duty to keep intouch with the people who made them leaders in the first place.*

BEYOND THE CALL

This is Uncle Sam's pay-day, and now that most of us have completed our annual 10-40 ritual, let's talk about Mrs. Joseph Kettering of Elizabethtown, Pennsylvania.

This lady has gone above and beyond the call of Internal Revenue Service.

Not only has Mrs. Kettering paid her tax bill, she's handed Uncle Sam a $20,000 tip. That's how much Mrs. Kettering sent to the federal government, to mark her seventieth birthday. With it, she sent a note, saying the money was a gift, in gratitude for being permitted to reach seventy in this great country.

She also sent Pennsylvania Governor Milton Shapp more than $2,000 . . . and Governor Nelson Rockefeller of New York $1,200 for the several years she spent, as she put it, "in your exciting state."

Well, such an unusual display of gratitude must have given IRS officials and those two governors a very warm feeling. But I'm sure somewhere within the government bureacracy, some computer is about to go out of its ever-lovin' electronic mind.

PASS THE PLATES

The California State Legislature raised $885,000.00 in just 9 months by offering personalized license plates. It's not an original concept; other states also have the so-called "vanity" plates which contain the driver's name, initials, telephone or house number. But only California, the state that gave us the Hollywood glossary, could turn a good idea into a super-stupendous, colossal success.

So, at $25 per plate, California lets motorists put any word, number or combination of words and numbers they want on their auto license plates. California cars now speed along the freeways bearing such tags as GIN, VODKA, PRIEST, TIGER, WOW and CRAZY. The list is endlessly varied, but the license officials do have to be careful. For instance, they caught one guy who ordered a meaningless combination of letters; only to the driver ahead, reading it in his rear view mirror, the word would not have been meaningless, it would have been obscene!

So, except for obscenities, a motorist can have just about any word he wants. HEAVEN has been taken, but so far, the license people haven't given anyone HELL, yet.

LAW AND THE CHANGING TIMES

Sometimes our cities seem to be ungovernable—our campuses, unmanageable.

Why? Is it because subversives have launched a concerted and coordinated campaign of confusion and disorder? Is it because both our cities and our universities have outgrown any meaningful control?

Certainly there are some who defy and disturb and destroy for the sheer satisfaction they seem to derive from it. But there may be a more significant and more wide-spread reason for the apparent lawlessness and disrespect which has been loosed in the land.

Judge Lester Maris of Newkirk, Oklahoma, unwittingly put his gavel on the problem when he ordered a woman reporter out of his courtroom because she was wearing a pants-suit.

True, pants-suits are socially acceptable now and the judge didn't argue that point. Citing an ancient rule against any courtroom attire for women except dresses, the Judge said, "We're sorry, but that rule was made before pants-suits came in."

Perhaps the ultimate test of our legal system will be how quickly the *laws can be changed* to meet the changing realities of our supersonically-paced society.

DIVORCE—FLORIDA STYLE

Divorce is never pleasant, but it doesn't always have to be tragic. Whether it is or not depends, in large measure, upon the law. Florida has taken a giant step toward making its divorce law more rational, and, as a result, more humane. Now, the only legal requirement for a divorce is that the court find the marriage irretrievably broken. Formerly, a Florida couple had to prove that one of them was either impotent, a drunk, a drug addict, had committed adultery or subjected the spouse to extreme cruelty. Often, a couple who simply recognized that their marriage wasn't working out, would have to decide which one would go into court and tell the damaging lie about the other one. It was always humiliating, and sometimes produced unnecessary bitterness and anger. It is still this way in many states.

Those who thought the liberalized divorce law would turn Florida into a divorce mill were wrong. What increase has occurred can be accounted for by population growth. As one divorce attorney puts it—the only guy who's been hurt by the new law is the private detective who used to make a bundle digging up domestic dirt.

VALUE: HUMAN VERSUS PROPERTY

The right to protect property is as American as apple pie. So, Donald Ceballos of San Rafael, California, probably believed he was well within his constitutional rights when he rigged a gun in his basement so it would go off automatically if anyone tried to break in.

Somebody did break in. Two teenaged boys. The booby-trap worked . . . and the older boy, a sixteen-year-old, was shot in the throat. He recovered. But Ceballos was brought to trial—and found guilty—of assault with a deadly weapon.

The prosecutor had argued that a spring-loaded gun such as Ceballos installed can't possibly distinguish between a burglar and anyone else. What if the house had caught fire while Ceballos was away and a fireman had broken in?

With break-ins on the increase, it's easy to understand the homeowner's concern for his property. But the jury apparently agreed with the prosecutor that any human life is more valuable than any piece of property. That, too, is a basic American concept.

RELIGION: TEACHING OR ESTABLISHING

It's been a decade, now, since the Supreme Court's ruling on prayer in public schools. Perhaps the smoke from that sizzling controversy has cleared, sufficiently, so that we can take a good, hard look at what was burned away and what was not.

For one thing, the High Court did *not* ban the Bible from classrooms. Many parents, as well as teachers and school administrators, thought it did. But, as one Washington woman noted recently, "without knowledge of religion you can't understand English literature, Middle East history, or the arts." She's right, of course. And the Supreme Court never intended that the Bible be abandoned as a literary and historical source.

In fact, just three years after the ruling, Justice Tom Clark wrote that a person's education is not complete without a study of comparative religion or the history of religion.

Perhaps the public finally is recognizing the subtle, but significant, *distinction* between teaching religion and establishing it. The Supreme Court has not ruled against the first. It has, I think wisely, upheld the constitutional provision which prohibits the second.

LAW TEMPERED BY MERCY

This is the story of a meter maid who may have done her job too well.

In Knoxville, Tennessee, a pick-up truck was parked outside the post office building. The man and woman who owned the old truck were inside the Salvation Army office, next door, picking up some badly needed clothing and bedding for themselves and their ten children. The ten children, ragged and obviously poor, were in the back of the truck, waiting for their parents, when along came this meter maid. She put a ticket on the truck's windshield.

Some federal employees, inside the Post Office, saw what happened. So, one of them went out, took the ticket off the truck, and wrote a letter to the police chief. The letter explained how furious the workers were at the meter maid for her lack of sensitivity. It went on to say, "If you feel this ticket must be paid, return it to us and we'll pay it immediately."

It can, of course, be argued that the meter maid was only doing her job of enforcing the law. The federal workers felt it was clearly a case where *justice* needed to be tempered by *mercy*.

DINNER WITH THE CHIEF

Getting a ticket from the police chief in Murray, Utah, may not be such a bad deal. It just might turn out to be a theatre ticket, complete with a complimentary dinner.

It started more than a year ago, when Police Chief Calvin Gillen and his wife invited 11-year-old Dee Dee Deniro to join them for dinner at a local restaurant. It was the Chief's way of saying "thank you" to Deniro, who had identified a burglary suspect. Later, the chief invited Tommy Randazzo to dinner. The seventeen-year-old Randazzo had pulled two girls from the flaming wreckage of a car.

Pretty soon, the idea caught on and became a tradition. Now, anyone in the small Salt Lake City suburb who performs some good deed, is a likely candidate for a dinner invitation from the chief. They also receive theatre tickets.

Four people are honored each month. There's no age limit: so far, they've ranged from seven to eighty-two years.

Chief Gillen started his "dinner-with-the-chief program" because he was concerned about people who had witnessed crimes, but refused to become involved. A lot of us are concerned about this problem. Congratulations to a police chief who's *doing* something about it.

HATS OFF TO THE ASHLAND COPS

Policemen, as a group, haven't exactly been at the top of the hero list with today's young people. But there's one group of officers in the tiny town of Ashland, Nebraska that should rate top honors from the teen set.

All five members of Ashland's force resigned because of what they considered a double-standard in the community; one code of conduct for the kids, another for adults.

The controversy reached a showdown after traffic radar was installed. Apparently, a lot of adults had the idea that radar would only be used to catch youthful speeders. They seemed to think that if an adult were stopped, he should not be given a ticket. The police thought otherwise. And, after Ashland's Mayor sided with a city council member against the police department's stand, all five officers—along with the police magistrate—quit! Double-standard radar is the kind of "establishment" hypocrisy that's turned a lot of young people off, where the "system" is concerned. This kind of courageous action, by five, fair-minded policemen, just might turn some of them on again.

SETTING THE RECORD STRAIGHT

Today, a personal observation—about welfare—and fraud. And one of the greatest frauds ever perpetrated upon the American public is the "big lie" about most recipients of public assistance. Politicians have gained countless points with their constituents by hammering away at the theme of "lazy, cheating, ne'er-do-wells, feeding endlessly at the government trough." Only, it isn't true, and anyone willing to look honestly at the statistics can *see* that it isn't true.

The latest study by the Department of Health, Education, and Welfare shows that, last year, only seven-tenths (.07) of one percent of those receiving welfare assistance, were even suspected of fraud. And state welfare officials could document actual fraud in only about half those suspected cases. Where fraud existed, it was often found that the person had a mental or physical problem, or that some special hardship did, in fact, exist.

This is not to suggest that all welfare recipients are one-hundred percent honest. But, then, name a group of human beings that is.

ON GENERALIZING

It's human nature, I suppose, to generalize about people. So, we embrace the myths that most welfare recipients could earn a living, that most young people have gone to pot, and that most politicians are self-serving.

There are, regrettably, some able-bodied ne'er-do-wells on public assistance rolls. But statistics show most simply are not qualified to work, even if jobs were available. Their handicap may be physical, or educational, or even lack of incentive—something their culturally deprived environment failed to provide.

Some young people do declare war on society, but most don't. And it well may be that apathy is still the greatest sin on the American campus.

Any newsman who has covered politicians will tell you that most are sincere, some are competent, and a few are even dedicated. After all, welfare recipients, young people, politicians—they really are no more different from the rest of us—than they are from each other.

POWER CORRUPTED

The clenched fist has become a symbol of our era, a symbol of determination, and power.

Political radicals use it—but they didn't invent it.

Long before Stokely Carmichael coined the phrase "black power," the sign of the clenched fist has been used by the establishment. My military service was spent in the Strategic Air Command, an outfit responsible for nearly all the Western world's nuclear fire power. The SAC symbol is a clenched fist, in a steel glove, clutching both olive branches and thunderbolts. The symbol, of course, suggesting that SAC uses its power for peace.

Power, in itself, is neither good nor bad. After all, nuclear energy can *light* a city as well as *level* one. The dictionary defines power simply as the ability to do, to act, to accomplish something. By this definition, who can seriously question the legitimacy of black power? ... or woman power? ... or power to the people?

Actually, the only power we need fear is power corrupted by hate. As a current bumper sticker puts it,

"You can't shake hands with a clenched fist."

THE MARKETPLACE

BUSINESS IS BETTER

The American businessman doesn't have to look far to find a critic these days. Consumers complain about inferior products, poor service, and planned obsolescence. Congress passes laws, while other governmental agencies issue rules, regulations, and guidelines, all aimed at reforming the machinery of commerce.

Environmentalists denounce business for polluting the air and water. Students berate the free enterprise system for a host of sins, ranging from the dehumanizing effects of technology to the excesses of advertising and appeals to greed.

Some of the criticisms are justified. Some are long overdue. But let's not be self-righteous in our judgment. To a degree, business is what we, the consumers, have made it. Today, when many corporations and business leaders are showing increasing sensitivity to society's problems, let's try to enlist business as a partner instead of using it as a scapegoat.

FRIENDLY COMPETITORS

Sometimes we see ourselves best through the eyes of others.

I saw a fresh demonstration of this truth during a visit, recently, to south Florida. I'd been invited to address a national trade convention. Mostly, it was American executives who were participating—but there were a couple of foreign businessmen attending as guests.

It was a rather typical convention, with the usual proportions of conferences and serious discussions on the one hand, and golf, fishing, swimming, and nightclubbing on the other. The participants were competitors in their field and this, it turned out, was what most impressed the foreign visitors.

They were utterly amazed to see the heads of giant corporations, accustomed to doing fierce battle on the field of business competition, not only sharing their professional concerns, but having a grand time together. We've always sort of taken it for granted in this country that competitors in commerce can be cordial and may be good friends. With a look of admiring bewilderment, one of the visiting executives said to me, "You know, this wouldn't be possible in my country."

LEARN BY DOING

Some time ago, a book was written outlining the so-called Peter principle. As I recall, that principle stated that a worker rises to the highest level of his own incompetence. In other words, about the time a fellow really learns a job, he gets promoted to an executive position for which he may not really possess the necessary skills. And, at the same time, his actual abilities are lost behind a desk.

Well, I'm not sure that Oregon's public school superintendent has come up with an antidote to the Peter principle . . . but he has got a darn good idea. Dale Parnell has decided to take a month off from his executive duties and spend that month in the classroom, teaching elementary school students. Parnell says he wants to find out what's going on in the primary grades, that he doesn't want to become isolated and lose touch. He wants to know what it's like for all those teachers who work under him.

Perhaps the proficiency level of all executives, in all walks of life, would be higher if, occasionally, they climbed down out of the executive suite and really found out what's going on below.

FACTORIES ARE CHANGING

Factories aren't the hum-drum, uninspiring dens of drudgery they used to be—at least, the best ones aren't. They've undergone some almost revolutionary changes, because the front office is learning that *humanization* can be just as important to productivity as *mechanization*.

Many managers are beginning to understand that human efficiency doesn't necessarily increase as tools and technology are improved. If the worker finds his job uninspiring or even repugnant, no amount of modernization is going to improve his morale. It may worsen it simply by underscoring his relative unimportance to the operation.

There are encouraging signs that white-collar management is coming to grips with the blue-collar blues, taking positive steps to dispel worker distrust of big organizations, encouraging greater worker participation in company goals. In general, they're trying to restore value to even the most routine task.

THEY NEED A UNION

According to a couple of consumer economists at Cornell, there's a class of worker in our society that's grossly overworked, underpaid, and probably, taken for granted. This group, numbering some 45-million, puts in an average of more than eight hours a day—seven days a week, the year round. It's not very glamorous work, either. There's some management and record keeping, but for the most part, the work consists of preparing food, cleaning up the after-meal mess, washing and ironing clothes, marketing, taking care of the children, and so forth. . . .

And what do these workers receive for their services? Usually not one cent—in direct wages. Because this work force is, technically, unemployed. It's the 45-million wives in the U.S. who have no outside jobs—the housewives. But they *do* work. So, these Cornell experts plan to use a government grant . . . and a computer . . . to figure out, in dollars and cents, just how much that work is worth.

And if we husbands thought the Women's Lib Movement was giving us a hard time, just wait until our wives all decide that what they really need . . . is a *union!*

HAVE CAKE AND EAT IT TOO?

Sometimes it's hard to tell which one wins the stupidity award—Management or Labor. Both sides have contributed their share to the antagonisms which create daily frictions and sometimes cause explosions at the bargaining table.

In Birmingham, Michigan, the award for pig-headedness undoubtedly goes to a local Teamsters Union. Or, perhaps it would be more fair to say, the union's local leadership.

80

Here's what happened: Intercontinental Steel Corporation agreed to let its workers put in ten hours a day for four days, instead of working eight hours a day for five. It still came out to forty hours, but it permitted the workers to enjoy a three-day weekend, instead of only two. It meant nothing to the company either way.

So what happens? Despite the fact that the workers loved the idea, their union leaders told management they'd have to start *paying time-and-a-half for those extra two hours a day*—the two hours which turned the eight hour day into a ten hour day!

Naturally, management didn't buy the have-cake-and-eat-it-too demand, so they simply ended the four-day week and put everybody back on a regular, old-fashioned, five-day week.

I don't think I would like to be one of those union leaders the next time a rank-and-file election comes up.

SEX SELLS—UNLESS IT'S ART

The story, date-lined Paramus, New Jersey, concerned a shopping center patronized by my family during our residency in New York—The Bergen Mall. That's why the story caught my eye. It told how art students at Fairleigh Dickinson University had been commissioned to cover an 800-foot wall along the Mall. And, under the supervision of their adviser, they produced some very stylized and unreal female forms. The nudes were not erotic in any way, certainly not obscene. But, some customers complained, so the manager of the Mall, David DeGhetto, ordered the murals covered with black paint.

Then came a most revealing comment. DeGhetto suggested that the nudes would have been appropriate in an art museum, but they didn't belong in a shopping center. "Promoting culture isn't our concern here," he said, "our business is retailing, getting people in for the merchants to take money."

DeGhetto's statement underscores one of the most important questions confronting 20th century society. Can any group—business or otherwise—continue to define its role along narrow, parochial lines of self-interest? Perhaps bread alone is not enough, even at the mall.

SHORT GUYS FINISH LAST

How about that survey showing that tall guys earn more starting salary than short fellows—no matter what they've got upstairs. According to the University of Pittsburgh's Leland Deck, men over 6-feet earn *substantially more* on their first job than the guys under six feet. Deck heads up Labor Relations in the school's Personnel Department. He claims a survey of Pitt Business School graduates in the late sixties showed men over 6-feet earning about 4% more than their shorter classmates. But, in 1970 a similar survey showed the percentage had jumped to 10%.

Deck believes there's a rather uncomplicated reason for this: The people who do the hiring, he figures, usually are not sophisticated enough to determine factors such as intelligence and motivation . . . but even a dimwitted employer can recognize if a guy is tall.

Doctor Deck isn't exactly sure what can be done about this obvious inequity. It's too subtle to be covered by present anti-discrimination laws. He does suggest that the short job-seeker might want to wear built-up heels . . . and . . . maybe tease his hair a little.

THE KILOS ARE COMING

We hear a lot about "changing the system." Well, somebody's about to change a system in America and *that* change is going to change our lives. I'm talking about the system we use for weighing and measuring— everything from turnpike distances to a quart of milk.

Right now, except for the United States, just about every other nation in the world has either switched from the "inch-pound" system to the **metric system,** or is in the process of making the switch. It's only logical that the United States get in step; international trade practically demands such uniformity.

What will it mean to us in practical, everyday terms when the switch is made? (Predictions are, it will be, by the end of this decade.) Well, *feet* will no longer be *feet,* they'll be **meters.** *Quarts* will be **liters** and *pounds* will be measured as **kilograms.**

It's really a lot more logical system since it's based on decimals—units of tens, hundreds, thousands. Compare this with the way we got our one-inch measurement; it dates back to the Middle Ages when an inch was supposed to be the approximate length of the first joint of the thumb! Not very scientific. Still, it is going to seem strange having a Miss America who measures 94-61-92.

BATHROOM ADS

Apparently, there's no limit to American ingenuity when it comes to spreading the sales message. Billboards—newspapers—magazines—television—radio— these conventional means for advertising products and services have been joined in recent years by matchcovers, bumper stickers, and miniature billboards in buses and on the rear-ends of taxi-cabs, blimps with flashing messages, and just recently, a ski-lodge began

83

selling advertising space on the back of ski-lift chairs. Now the skier can sit frozen to his chair while reading such messages as ... "Don't you wish you were in Miami?"

But the top prize for innovative sponsorship has got to go to a firm which is now selling advertising in office building rest-rooms! The humorous possibilities, if you'll pardon my saying so, of this johnny-come-lately advertising medium . . . the *possibilities* boggle the mind. At the very least, perhaps the creative talent employed by America's advertising agencies will be able to improve the quality of rest-room *graffiti*.

BEAUTY AND THE BUSINESS-BEAST

In 1967, the United States House of Representatives got into the beauty business. The woman who had operated the House Beauty Shop Concession for thirty years got mad and walked out ... lock, stock, and hair-dryer.

Well, the women who work on Capitol Hill *had* to have a place where they could be "done-over" from time to time, so, the House voted $15,000 from its Contingency Fund to set up its own beauty parlor. The job of running it was turned over to a special committee, and, by the end of the first year, the House-operated beauty parlor had paid back **half** of the investment! The next year, it paid the remaining $7,500; and in 1970—business was so good—the shop handed Congress a check for eight thousand dollars, in lieu of rent!

Although it's open to the public, most of the beauty shop's customers are Congresswomen, secretaries, and other female staff-members on the Hill.

The chairman of the committee which runs the shop is Representative Martha Griffiths of Michigan. She says it's the only thing around Capitol Hill that's operating in the black . . . and, she says *it's the only thing being operated by women.* You think she's trying to tell us something?

TAPPING THE TECHNICAL POOL

The White House has taken one small step toward solving the problem of mass lay-offs in the space industry. (Hopefully, some great leaps will follow.) The small step is a million-dollar experimental program designed to help unemployed engineers and scientists find jobs where they're needed; namely, in new urban planning projects with local and state governments.

Initially, it's expected that about 400 highly-trained people will benefit from the computerized placement program. Most will be former aerospace or defense industry employees—victims of a shrinking Space budget and a generally sluggish economy. As good as it is, this program will barely make a dent in the overall problem. *It's estimated that some 60,000 high-level scientists and engineers are out of work!*

Perhaps, if the experiment succeeds, it can be expanded. Given our present, and future, problems of population, pollution, and production, it would be tragic if this reservoir of talent went down the drain—and new talent refused to jump into the scientific pool.

WHERE THE NEED IS

It hasn't been so terribly long ago that a teaching certificate was an automatic meal-ticket in the U.S. Schools and colleges seemed to have an insatiable appetite for qualified instructors; and, while they didn't get rich, teachers always were assured of a job. Not anymore. At Berkshire Community College in Massachusetts, for instance, more than *16-hundred people* applied for the school's *twelve* teaching vacancies. Only 15-hundred youngsters applied for the 750 student openings. And Berkshire's situation is typical. Suddenly, even Ph.D.'s have become a glut on the teacher market.

Well, some of the nation's unemployed teachers have found that their services are still highly prized in other parts of the world . . . Australia, for example. A group of 110 American teachers has flown to Australia, with the Australian government picking up their air fares, and they've got two-year contracts waiting for them. Perhaps we are witnessing a reversal of the so-called "brain drain," which has worried foreign governments for years. Maybe Uncle Sam is about to make good on a long overdue talent debt.

JUST WHAT WE NEED

Necessity may be the mother of invention but I suspect she's not very proud of some of her offspring. Take, for instance, that new sandbox for cats—the one with the automatic drain; or, that invention displayed by a biology professor in Paris—he calls it a "cubicle for biological regeneration through microvibration with hyperactive geomagnetic waves emitted by volatile mineral salts." I'm afraid to ask what it is, but it sounds like something almost any home could do without.

Now, the guy who recently invented those zig-zag metal strips for balconies or roof ledges—the ones designed to protect pedestrians from pigeon fallout—he may have something. Then there is the fellow who designed desk drawers which shut, automatically, the moment a girl leaves her desk. *That* could save countless pairs of nylon stockings.

Well, I've got an invention of my own which I'm prepared to discuss with any serious backer: it's a coffee dispenser which looks exactly like a filing cabinet. (A perfect match for all those coffee drinkers who look exactly like office workers.)

Some Personal Observations on . . .
RELIGION

OBJECTIVITY

Someone asked me, the other day, if a newsman could hold any specific religious beliefs and still be an objective journalist. Is it possible, he wondered, for a reporter to accept any personal philosophy or theology and still remain unbiased as he views life and reports it.

Like so many questions, it sounds reasonable—until we take it apart. If commitment to certain ideals precludes a newsman from giving a fair shake to opposing concepts, then, perhaps, we must also conclude that a married newsman could not impartially cover a divorce proceeding; or, that a female reporter could not report objectively on abortion; or, that a newsman with school-age children could not be fair in his coverage of a PTA meeting.

We all wear many hats, play many roles, and function in many ways. Objectivity and fairness are not products of roles we play, these qualities come from a state of mind . . . an attitude. Indeed, an honest faith, born of commitment to truth, might well be one's best hope for genuine objectivity.

TAKING THE CHURCH'S TEMPERATURE

American churches are spending more now, but probably enjoying it less. That's because *most* of what the churches are spending is going back into their own self-perpetuating programs, such things as building maintenance, staff salaries, and services provided for the direct benefit of church members. Despite the clear Christian teaching that the church exists to serve the world, most churches seem to be serving themselves first. The world gets what's left over, and it's usually not very much.

A survey, by the National Council of Churches, shows that nearly 79% of all money contributed to American churches is spent on their internal programs. Just over twenty-one percent goes for outside benevolences, such things as missions, hospitals, orphanages, ghetto projects, and the like.

The major denominations seem to be the worst offenders. Episcopalians, Southern Baptists, and United Methodists, for example, channel only about 15% of their funds to uses outside their own congregations. And, just in case you're keeping score, the Seventh Day Adventists have the best record: 72% for benevolences!

CRISIS OF FAITH

When leaders of the United Church of Christ met in Grand Rapids, Michigan, they took a long hard look at what the church ought to be doing in the days ahead. They used, as the basis for their considerations, a 2-year study by a Special Council of Mission Priorities.

That council interviewed church members all over the country, trying to find out what issues and concerns they, the members, felt should receive *priority attention* from the church. The grass-roots study showed the members troubled by four basic concerns: the need for racial justice now; peace, and the redirection of American power; revitalization of the local church; and the need for a renewed faith.

To see church leaders zeroing-in on such issues would be encouraging, but to see the people in the pews come to grips with these important challenges is downright inspiring. Historically, the most dynamic movements always have been those where the *people were moved* to act. If renewal comes to the modern church, or, for that matter, to democratic society, it will be because the people demand it—not because the leaders declare it.

OVERCOMING THE EDIFICE COMPLEX

Today, the story of a church that really took Christianity seriously. It's a Methodist church at Tyrone, Pennsylvania, where massive layoffs at the town's biggest factory put more than 500 people out of work.

Eight years ago, the Columbia Avenue Methodist church lost its building in a fire. Since then, the congregation has worshiped in makeshift quarters, striving together and saving for their Building Fund—and looking forward to having their own church again. They were just about ready to put up the brand new building when the unemployment crisis hit the community. But, instead, the church has turned over to a local Community Improvement Corporation $100,000 of its building fund money.

The loan means Tyrone will be able to make a serious bid for new industry—perhaps initiate a one-million-dollar industrial development project. But, it also means, the Columbia Avenue Methodist Church will have to delay building their new sanctuary. The pastor, Leroy J. Harrison, doesn't think the church's response to the town's need is so unusual. Harrison says it's simply something the Christian Gospel demands that his people do.

PASSING THE BUCK

When members contribute to a church, that's not news; but when a church contributes to its members, that's news. And that's exactly what the United Methodist Church of West Springfield, Massachusetts, has done.

The Reverend Robert Sweet, Jr., surprised his 175 parishioners one Sunday by passing a basket filled with brand new one-dollar bills, and asking each member to take one.

Then, he urged each to take their dollar, invest it in something, and return their profits to the church. Now, the members who didn't make it to church that Sunday didn't get off the hook, their dollar was sent to them through the mail. Altogether, the Reverend Sweet sent out about $500 in hopes his members will take seriously the parable of the talents and use their sacred trust for the growth and ultimate enrichment of others.

In passing the bucks, the Reverend Sweet said he had only one real concern: . . . that he might find all those new bills showing up the following Sunday in the collection plate.

OLD MYTH/NEW REALITY

Another old myth has given way to a new reality. This time, the myth-slayers are Thomas Campbell, Associate Professor of Church and Community at Chicago Theological Seminary, and, Yoshio Fukuyama, Professor of Religious Studies at Pennsylvania State University. They surveyed 8,000 upper-middle-class Protestants to see if there's any correlation between personal piety and social concern.

Now, it's always been presumed, by many liberals, both inside and outside the church, that as personal devotion goes up, involvement with such social causes as civil rights goes down.

Not so, according to the survey. Those who observed such pietistic practices as daily prayer and devotional reading, scored substantially higher than others in their willingness to, for instance, accept members of a minority group as next-door neighbors. The devotionalists, as they're sometimes scornfully called by the activists, also scored higher where support for social justice is concerned.

Even the two liberal sociologists, who conducted the survey, admit they were astonished to find that religious piety actually increases concern for social issues.

THE FORBIDDEN TOPIC

Let's look at a forbidden topic—Death. Time was when people *openly discussed death*—and *sex was obscene*. Now, according to a University of Iowa professor, it's the other way around! Sex is openly discussed in our society . . . but death is obscene. Doctor David Belgum says this has serious implications for the person who is dying. He may wish to discuss it with his family or friends, but often he can't find anyone willing to listen. You see, we've tried to pretend death doesn't happen. And failing to face up to it merely complicates the problem posed by death.

Anthropologist Margaret Mead says many of modern man's anxieties result from the fact that no matter how many other problems are banished—hunger, violence, or whatever—man knows he cannot banish death. Facing the fact can help us to make right choices and to use wisely the limited time available to us. Trying to ignore death can bind us up with a thousand useless worries. Since death is every bit as much a part of life as sex, perhaps it deserves at least as much recognition.

CHURCH TURNS THEM ON

As buildings grow taller and spaceships fly higher, man's image of himself seems to soar. As man's own self-esteem rises, his image of a Greater Power behind it all tends to shrink. This is especially true for young people.

Adolescence is a time for flexing one's own muscles, for sensing one's innate powers; youthful rejection of religion is, at least partly, physiological. But given a religious framework which **challenges** without belittling, even young people can be turned on by the church.

It's happening . . . all across the country. And those churches willing to recognize what a contribution their cocky, self-assured youngsters *can* make, are finding many of the kids ready and willing to contribute.

I know of one Presbyterian Church which has ordained an 18-year-old elder . . . and a Congregational Church, near Minneapolis, with a deacon and a deaconess who are 15 years of age. Perhaps this will be the decade when churches stop asking . . . "what can we do for our youth" . . . and begin asking . . . what can we do WITH THEM?

RELEVANT AND REVERENT

For those Americans who fear Congress has become a "den of thieves" and a "haven for irreligious scoundrels," few statistics are actually available on the number of thieves who win House seats, and there are no current figures on the number of scoundrels, either. But evidence has come to light that Congress is **not** irreligious!

Room H-234 is hardly noticed by the tourist trekking through the Capitol rotunda. But, behind that closed, unmarked door is a *prayer room*—a quiet room with two plain prayer benches, an opened Bible, and seats for ten.

Although the Constitution prohibits any law establishing religion, it also prohibits any impediment or abridgment of the free exercise of religion. So, in the mid-fifties, Room H-234 was set aside for Congressmen to pray, or simply to meditate.

It's estimated that from 50- to 60 members of Congress use the room each working day. That's only about 10% of the lawmakers who *could* use it. But, hopefully, God can do business without a quorum!

Some Personal Observations on . . .
LIFE STYLES
and
HAPPINESS

MUHAMMAD'S WISDOM

To be young, black, boastful, and successful, is to be controversial. Add to all that an unpopular religious belief, plus public defiance of the military draft, and you have an emotionally explosive combination.

In a word, you have Muhammad Ali, former world heavyweight boxing champ, stripped of his title, convicted of draft evasion, sentenced to the Federal pen, then exonerated by the United States Supreme Court—without dissent. That decision will be debated by Ali's critics and fans for years to come. Just as the decision to take away his title continues to generate verbal fireworks.

But admirers—and detractors—are a dime a dozen. And what must be really important to Ali is what he thinks about himself. Whatever else he is, Ali is a sensitive young man, whose sincerity finally convinced the nation's highest court. Throughout the entire ordeal, Clay insisted he was just "doing his purpose" . . . that was his own phrase. Maybe we'd all be better off if we'd be less concerned with doing our *thing,* and more concerned with doing our *purpose.*

IF YOU'RE SO RICH . . . HOW COME . . .

There's a sign you can buy at roadside gift shops which says, "If you're so smart, why ain't you rich?" Bad grammar—but a good question. Here's another good question: If you're so rich, why aren't you happy?

It's a good question, because, according to several recent surveys, most Americans are not happy, despite the fact that we live in luxury undreamed of in other eras and other cultures.

John Cunniff, Associated Press writer, put his finger on the problem when he noted that the desires of most people are never satisfied. Goals, he says, are only beads in a string that never runs out.

So, the typical American family works long and hard to buy a nice home—only to discover that what they want then, is a vacation home. They purchase a good car—then realize that what they really need is a second car, or a boat—or, well, the list grows longer with each new acquisition.

18,000,000 wives now work; that's 40% of America's married women. Most don't work for professional satisfaction or personal fulfillment, they work to maintain a standard of living which, somehow, never seems to be quite high enough. For most people, "the good life" remains a GOAL—forever just out of reach.

BIG CITY BLUES

Remember the World War I song—"How you gonna keep 'em down on the farm, after they've seen Par-ee?" Well, THAT isn't the problem anymore. The challenge facing big corporations today is: how you gonna get 'em into the big cities, after they've tasted the easier, less frantic life offered by smaller communities?

Executive recruiters frankly admit they're having a

98

tough time luring promising young talent into America's teeming urban centers. One talent scout said he was doing fine until he mentioned that the location of the high-paying executive job was New York, then, he lost half his candidates.

Good salaries, night life, the arts—these used to draw ambitious young people to New York, Chicago and Los Angeles, the way cheese attracts rats. Today poor commuting, high taxes, and pollution are making the rat-race less attractive.

It's just possible that the lure of smaller cities, such as Louisville, also means more people are beginning to give as much thought to personal and family values as they do to their careers.

OUR BROTHER'S KEEPER

One of the most tragic by-products of urbanization is the way it insulates and isolates people. The sense of interpersonal responsibility for our fellowman seems to shrink in direct proportion to the growth of our cities.

There was a fresh reminder of this recently, in Detroit, when the grief-stricken mother of a little girl, killed by a hit-and-run driver, *pleaded,* unsuccessfully, with her neighbors, to identify the man at the wheel. Mrs. Portia Redmond says several witnesses have told her, privately, they know who did it. But they refused to tell the police. Six-year-old Sonyra Redmond and her cousin, three-year-old LaRhonda Bush, were run down and killed as they crossed a street toward an ice cream truck. All the witnesses to the tragedy have clammed up —they don't want *to get involved*!

America's moral softness is not seen nearly so clearly in the flag-burning obscene chanting of a few, as it is in the apathy and the indifference of many.

EVERYONE NEEDS A TREEHOUSE

Why does a boy love a treehouse? Our five-year-old spends hours, alone with his thoughts and his imaginary friends, on a small slab of plywood nailed to the top of two crooked tree limbs. It took me a long time to figure out why he retreats to that little hide-away instead of to his toy-filled playroom, his gadget-filled bedroom, or a dozen other seemingly more desirable places.

The answer came one day watching my neighbor and his wife pack a tent in the trunk of their car, preparing for a weekend in the woods. Why in the world would any sensible couple leave an air-conditioned home, with color-TV and indoor plumbing, to fight mosquitos, spend a restless night in a lumpy sleeping bag, and put up with other inconveniences their ancestors spent centuries trying to overcome?

It's really not such a hard question to answer. Whether our choice is a boat on some secluded lake, a vacation home in the mountains, or, as in my case, a small airplane flying high above the routine restrictions and demands of life . . . the fact is . . . nobody ever completely outgrows his need for a treehouse.

SIDEWALKS

Following a Heart Association meeting in New York City, famed cardiologist, Doctor Paul Dudley White, decided to walk the several miles to LaGuardia airport. He was somewhat perturbed to discover that the Queensboro bridge, connecting Queens and Manhattan, had no pedestrian walkway. So he was forced to take a bus across the bridge.

It's ironic, in an era when we are becoming more conscious of the need to exercise, the opportunities for walking seem to be steadily diminishing. Many of our newest suburbs are created without sidewalks. Often those of us who would prefer walking find ourselves forced to take the car, simply because walkways aren't available.

Shortly after moving into our present home, I decided to walk to the drugstore—a short distance of only a block and a half. But most of the time, I found myself walking in the street, or on the edge of someone's lawn.

Not only is walking about the best form of exercise we can get, it's also a small step toward reducing automobile air pollution. While Detroit is designing engines which pollute less, our city engineers should consider bringing back that old-fashioned, but still needed facility—the sidewalk.

ANOTHER WORRY

The list of human activities branded as DANGEROUS, continues to grow. Now, to cigarette smoking, over-eating, and consumption of contaminated seafoods, we can add another potentially harmful indulgence—driving too fast.

Oh, I don't mean the usual danger which speeding creates—the risk of wrapping your car around a tree or slamming into another car; I mean the danger to your health posed by driving fast.

British medical researchers have determined that motorists who ride with a heavy foot on the accelerator may be speeding toward heart disease. Speeding generates excitement; that generates fatty acids in the blood. Fatty acids accumulate on artery walls, leading to arteriosclerosis and, possibly, heart disease. The researchers base their conclusions on tests of racing drivers—before and after major racing events. The tests reveal high increases of certain fatty substances, associated with heart disease, during the races.

Obviously, other kinds of emotional stress—such as competition on the job—can do the same thing. So, the word for the day is: WARNING—racing your motor, or your car's motor, may be hazardous to your health.

TALENT CONSERVATION

Ed Caldwell earns nearly twenty-thousand dollars a year . . . as a stock boy in a Tullahoma, Tennessee, grocery store! He used to earn the same salary as a civilian engineer for the United States Air Force. Caldwell was one of thousands of highly trained personnel who got caught in the economy-squeeze which eliminated a lot of top jobs. With 22 years of government work behind him, Caldwell wasn't anxious to quit civil service; besides, government regulations permitted him to take the stock boy job (in the commissary at the engineering center) *at no loss in pay,* for at least two years!

Normally, that stock job pays a top salary of just under $5700—less than ⅓ of what Caldwell is receiving. I suppose a lot of white-collared executives and professional men have wondered what it would be like to have a less demanding job—at the same high pay. Wouldn't it be great to give up the pressure, the tough decision-making, but still earn top management income?

Well, it isn't working that way for Ed Caldwell. He's learning one of life's great truths—that happiness doesn't come by fleeing responsibility, but by meeting it —head-on. Caldwell says he wants back in engineering just as soon as he can get there.

FULFILLMENT

Sometimes the grass really *is* greener on the other side of the fence. Sometimes the only way to be sure is to switch sides. David Sachs did. And Sachs says he's happier now than he's ever been in his life.

After earning his B.S. degree with honors—an M.D. at Stanford—spending six years residency at UCLA and Johns Hopkins—and serving two years as an Air Force flight surgeon—Sachs became chief-of-surgery at Los Angeles Veterans hospital. Then, for five years, he was in private practice, published several research papers, and performed more than 400 operations. Sounds like a fulfilling career, doesn't it? There was just one problem: Dr. Sachs didn't really want to be a doctor. What he *really* wanted to be—what he'd always wanted to be—was an actor!

So, now he's an actor. Now 38, Sachs has appeared in three movies, including the comedy, M*A*S*H (in which he played a surgeon), and eight TV dramas. Sachs hasn't quit medicine entirely, though—he teaches heart and lung surgery at UCLA. But acting is his first love. And even though he earned more as a doctor, Sachs has learned that reaching the top of the ladder doesn't mean much—if you've leaned the ladder against the wrong wall.

SEARCH FOR MEANING

During a farewell party for President Johnson and other visiting chiefs-of-state at the Manila summit conference a few years ago, a colleague from another network said to me, "Mort, it's a great life, isn't it?" We were all groggy with fatigue, almost too tired to enjoy the royal dinner and dance given by President and Mrs. Ferdinand Marcos. But my friend's point was clear: as newsmen, covering the Presidential beat, life was vibrant, exciting, full of meaning.

Not all news assignments are exhilarating, but there's little boredom in this business. Of course, we've all met people with apparently interesting jobs who found them dull. Maybe it's a matter of *finding the meaning* that exists in almost any work. Sometimes it requires a vocational change; witness comedian Bill Cosby's decision to give up a glamorous, show-business career and become a teacher; or, rock guitarist Tom Fogarty's defection from the Creedence Clearwater Revival group so he can give more time to his family.

Happiness . . . is many jobs. And no job . . . is a guarantee of fulfillment.

A FORM OF SUICIDE

Man grasps for immortality in many ways . . . by having children . . . or by some monumental achievement worthy of the history books . . . or by creating a work of art; for art is, truly, an extension of the human personality.

When a work of art is destroyed, something of the creator's soul dies too. So, what could possibly motivate an artist to deliberately destroy the work it took him years to create? Take Max Epstein, for instance, a Canadian artist whose talents with a brush far exceeded his skill as a businessman.

Despite a growing reputation, Epstein was hopelessly in debt. When a Montreal bank announced it would take possession of Epstein's paintings from a downtown gallery, Epstein got there first and chopped the canvases into shreds with an ax. Why such senseless destruction? Epstein says he "couldn't bear to see the work of a lifetime acutioned off, like so many used cars." One can only pity Epstein for his desperate act of self-destruction; it was, for him, no doubt, a form of suicide.

BETTER TO GIVE

It is better to give than to receive. To most of us, that's a nice thought—a worthy sentiment, perhaps— but to Ed and Claire Manwell, it's a proven principle. For nearly ten years, the Manwells have been globe-trotting for a few weeks each year, sharing their skills and themselves with the less fortunate.

Both Ed and Claire are doctors. He's a surgeon; she's a retired pediatrician. But periodically Ed leaves his practice in Northhampton, Massachusetts and Claire comes out of retirement and they take their much-needed medical knowledge and instruments to places such as Kenya, Nigeria, Guinea, or Vietnam. They've doctored needy Navajos on Arizona reservations. During the Biafran war, they took care of thousands of starving children, and built a hospital from scratch. Ed performed surgery under the glare of a detached car headlight hooked to a battery.

Both in their mid-sixties, the Manwells say they do this instead of taking vacations. We might think about that the next time we plan that annual orgy of expensive self-indulgence we call a vacation. Is it possible the Manwells know something we don't about *enjoyment*?

PUTTING MONEY WHERE THE MOUTH IS

It's one thing to stand up and say what you believe. It's quite another thing to back up that statement with action. But sometimes . . . somebody does, and recently, a couple of Americans did just that.

Doctor David Baltimore, a 33-year-old Minneapolis cancer researcher refused to keep a $1000 prize awarded him by a drug firm. Why? Dr. Baltimore believes the drug industry is making exorbitant profits at the expense of those who can least afford it . . . the sick and the infirm. To back up his protest, Baltimore gave his prize money to scientific investigators who are working in the public interest.

The other man willing to back up his profession in practice is William Guthrie, the airline captain who was fired for refusing to dump jet fuel into the atmosphere. The federal government wanted to present him an award for his courage, but Guthrie refused it. He said the offer is clear indication the government, too, regards "dumping" an unacceptable procedure. And Guthrie believes his greatest reward would be for the government to force an end to such pollution. From now on, when Dr. Baltimore or Captain Guthrie talks about his convictions—people are going to listen.

AND MANY HAPPY RETURNS

Simon Solomon and his wife, Charlotte, live in the Detroit suburb of Livonia. Their birthdays are just a day apart, so, traditionally they've celebrated together. This year they'd planned a trip. Then, for some reason, Simon and Charlotte got a better idea: this year, instead of doing something for each other, they decided to do something for somebody else.

So, they invited thirty-one boys from the Starr Commonwealth Home in Adrian to be their guests at lunch. Then, they took all 31 youngsters to an afternoon performance of Pinocchio.

It was a day those boys are likely to remember for a long, long time. The Starr Commonwealth Home has 200 boys, ranging in age from 10 to 15. Some are from broken homes, some have been referred by juvenile courts throughout Michigan—most are orphans.

Perhaps Simon and Charlotte Solomon have finally come up with the ideal gift idea . . . for that person . . . who has everything.

ONE-MAN VICE SQUAD

United States customs inspectors are hard to shock. They've seen just about everything. But the guys who keep an eagle-eye on traffic across the United States/Mexican border were not quite prepared for the bizarre case of non-smuggling they ran into when an American showed up on the Mexican side . . . with ninety-three pounds of marijuana! He didn't try to hide it. In fact, he declared it! Then told customs officials he had deliberately purchased the pot in Mexico just so it could be kept off the American market and out of the hands of his fourteen children.

The man apparently didn't want any publicity. He asked that his name not be released. However, customs officials did check out his story. After confirming it, all they could do was say "thank you" and let the man cross on back to the United States side.

That ninety-three pounds of pot would have brought from $14,000 to $16,000 on the streets of America's cities. Officials don't know what the non-smuggler paid for it. Apparently, somebody forgot to tell that one-man vice squad that individuals don't count anymore.

THE LAST MEASURE

Some men horde their worldly goods until the very end; then, in a final bid to purge their greed, bequeath their possessions to some charity or public foundation. But for other men, generosity is a way of life . . .

And that's how it was with Charles Schaake of Seattle. Charles wasn't a wealthy man. He lived comfortably, selling groceries from his little corner store. But the way Charles ran his business, he never had a chance to get rich. For one thing, he gave too many groceries away to those who couldn't pay. And, he sold a lot on

107

credit. Charles had a very poor memory, too, especially if he knew his debtor was hard up and unable to pay. Oh yes, that delivery service operated at a loss—the one Charles Schaake ran for the benefit of the elderly and the ill.

So, knowing the kind of man Charles was in life, his customers and other friends weren't at all surprised to learn that Charles' last thought was for others. Just before he died, from bullet wounds, inflicted by a young robber, Charles asked that the last 800-dollars worth of canned goods on his shelves be given to Seattle's poor.

Charles Schaake . . . a grocer . . . who did not live . . . by bread alone.

SECOND FIDDLE

Music hath charm to soothe the savage beast. But, it also has the demonstrated ability to teach discipline. No less a public person than President Nixon has paid homage to music's character-building power.

The President told a conference of music educators in Atlantic City that he owes much of his own speaking ability to his musical background. Mr. Nixon said the discipline of practicing, rehearsing, and memorizing music, helped him immeasurably when he had to face an audience and speak. In fact, the President is quoted as having said . . . "To the extent that I can now face an audience without referring to written notes, the experience and discipline of performing music in high school must be given first credit."

We did a little research and discovered that Richard Nixon played second violin in his high school orchestra. Later, you may recall, he played second chair under President Eisenhower. And while he didn't specifically mention it, we suspect that President Nixon, like the rest of us, probably learned a few good lessons—from playing—"second fiddle."

MARRIAGE IS ALIVE AND WELL

It's been said you can prove anything with statistics. And statistically, the divorce rate is rising. Some say this proves that marriage is a dying institution, but marriage expert Jean Stone says—nonsense. She says it's growing pains, not the death grip that is wrenching this age-old custom called marriage. Mrs. Stone has spent years studying marriages. She's interviewed men of all ages, at all economic levels, and she's found that the normal, healthy male of the '70's, no less than his counterpart of a century ago, still looks to marriage for affection, understanding, comradeship, and above all, freedom from competition. There's so much competition for a man out in the world, he desperately seeks security in the haven of his marriage.

But the institution is changing. For one thing, young women are no longer under social or family pressures to marry young. It's now acceptable for them to get an apartment, take a job, go to college, and take a little time to mature. And Jean Stone believes this trend will make today's single girl a better, more assured, prospect for that life-time contract.

MOE'S DAY IN COURT

Jim and Donna Davis had no children. They longed for the pitter-patter of little feet. So, Jim and Donna adopted a three-year-old by the name of Moe.

The next thing they knew—Jim, Donna, and their new little dependent were all three in court. Neighbors in their Los Angeles suburb of West Covina had complained about Moe. Not that he was noisy . . . Moe was extremely well-mannered, anyone could see that, just watching Moe in the courtroom. In fact, he seemed better behaved than the average three-year-old.

It was obvious Moe was getting good treatment. Dressed in a little checkered shirt, white trousers and shoes, Moe was a handsome little monkey—I should say, "handsome little *chimp*"—because Moe is a trained chimpanzee. A chimp so civilized he brushes his teeth and uses the toilet; again—outstanding behavior for any three-year-old. But a community ordinance says "no wild animals may be kept" in West Covina, and technically, Moe is a wild animal. Fortunately, the judge was so impressed by Moe's exemplary conduct, he threw the case out of court! Moe promptly sauntered up to the bench, and shook the judge's hand.

SPACE HERO

Astronaut Joe Engle may never make the history books, but he does deserve a footnote for his courage and his character. His courage may never be tested on the moon, but it's already been demonstrated on the rugged terrain of disappointment.

For 6 long years Engle planned, trained and hoped for a Moon Mission. He'd been a crack test pilot, flying the experimental X-15 to the very fringes of space. Then he became an astronaut and finally was selected to fly Apollo 17 . . . the last Moon Mission.

Then, suddenly, came the devastating news that he'd been "bumped" from the flight. NASA had decided to send a scientist-astronaut on the final Moon landing—geologist Jack Schmitt.*

Engle must have felt as Adlai Stevenson did when he

*Broadcast on September 23, 1971.

lost the Presidential election . . . "too old to cry, but it hurts too much to laugh." Still, at his news conference, Engle displayed no self-pity but said he would do everything possible to help make the mission a success.

We need guys like Joe Engle to remind us, now and then, what it means to be a good loser.

Some Personal Observations on . . .
WHAT'S HAPPENING
(and other random thoughts ! !)

HOW TO CURE ANYTHING?

Compulsive gambling is more than a problem in Sydney, Australia, it's almost an epidemic. Officials estimate that slot machines in the Sydney area take in more than one and three-quarter-billion dollars every year. Now, some Australian psychiatrists have developed a shock treatment to help gambling addicts shun the one-armed bandits.

"Aversion Therapy" is used when normal psychiatric treatment, and pills, have failed. It produces results about 60% of the time—and here's how it works: A regular slot machine is wired so that while a customer—in this case, a patient—is playing it, he periodically gets an electrical shock. The shock may be as high as ninety volts, and he never knows when it's coming. Some patients are reduced to tears. One man got down on his knees and begged to be excused from ever pulling the slot-machine's arm again.

Well, what I'm waiting for is shock-treatment for addiction to fudge, and pies, and doughnuts. Maybe those of us who have to count calories would do a better job if the fattening things we bit into . . . *bit back*.

CALORIES DO COUNT . . . BUT . . .

I was never quite able to convince myself that calories don't count—despite that book to the contrary. Or, rather, they always seemed to add up on my body. I am convinced that Doctor T. C. McDaniel is on the right dietary track when he contends that it's the *quality* —not the *quantity*—of food that determines whether you put weight on or take it off.

McDaniel, who practices in Cincinnati, told a medical meeting recently that many of his patients lose weight eating up to five meals a day. And, they eat a lot of food. They never go hungry. The trick is in knowing **what** to eat. He recommends fruits, vegetables, honey, and meat. No fats or starches; in other words, eat lots of wholesome, nutritious foods which fill you up—not out.

Long before Dr. McDaniel revealed his success with this method, I had learned, first hand, how much more successful a diet is which doesn't leave the dieter wracked with hunger pains. For me, the McDaniel system works. And in dieting, IT'S NOT HOW YOU PLAY THE GAME THAT COUNTS—BUT WHETHER YOU GAIN OR LOSE.

DO THE THING YOU FEAR

Today, a word about fear. Three British doctors claim they've discovered a new method for treating phobias . . . for helping people overcome their fears. It's really quite simple. The patient is merely required to *do* the thing he fears. For instance, one young man who had been afraid of balloons . . . since childhood . . . was put in a room full of balloons. For nearly an hour, doctors went around bursting the balloons, and the young man left the room cured of his fear.

In an article in the British Medical Journal, these same

114

doctors—J. P. Watson, R. Gaind, and I. M. Marks—
tell how a 20-year-old secretary overcame her lifelong
fear of cats . . . by spending four hours in a room with a
black cat. By the time the session was over, the cat was
purring peacefully on the girl's lap, and she was petting
it.

The idea of conquering fear by doing the thing you're
afraid of is a good idea—but it's not new. The British
doctors, it would seem, have simply adapted an old
principle to the treatment of personal phobias. People
have always feared what they did not understand. The
concept is as old as sun-worshiping.

TECHNOLOGY FOR HEALTH

It's time for a re-evaluation of our modern technology . . . that favorite whipping boy of sociologists and
ecologists, who sometimes seem to blame technology for
all modern man's problems.

It's true, science and technology did bring us the hydrogen bomb. It's true that, in the name of progress,
we've managed to dirty up our air and water. However,
before we engage in too much wistful reminiscing about
the "good old pre-scientific days," before we drown ourselves in sentimental tears for the pre-technological existence of our ancestors, let's put the problem into perspective.

Early next month, at a medical-equipment exhibit in
Australia, some new computerized equipment will be
demonstrated which could save countless heart disease
victims. In the demonstration, experts at the Mayo Clinic
in Rochester, Minnesota, will read an electro-cardio-
gram *being transmitted live 10,000 miles from Sydney!*
The success of this "health hot-line" could mean that
someday, everyone on earth, no matter how remote his
town or village, will be within immediate reach of the

best medical advice in the world. That's technology at its best.

WHICH IS WITCH, DOCTOR?

Every generation, I suppose, possesses a certain arrogance about its accomplishments—its progress—its superior knowledge. We all have a tendency to look down our collective noses at the quaint mannerisms, naive methods, and limited understanding of our forebears. But, occasionally, something happens to remind us we aren't so terribly smart, after all.

More than once, medical science has come around to the conclusion that grandma really did know best. It may have taken modern medical science to tell us why her remedies were effective. But that is analysis—not discovery.

Now, according to Doctor E. Fuller Torrey of the National Institute of Mental Health, even psychiatry isn't all that new. Most of us tend to date the birth of psychoanalysis with the work of Sigmund Freud. Dr. Torrey says several years of studying healers in other cultures shows that the techniques employed by western psychotherapists are about the same as those used for centuries . . . by witch doctors.

SOLVING THE DOCTOR SHORTAGE

Periodically, a news item crosses my desk telling of some small town's fruitless search for a doctor. There are many communities in the United States with a critical shortage of doctors, and some without a single M.D.

Now, a couple of medical students may have come up with just the right prescription. In fact, if the plan Sol Edelstein and Douglas Jackson have worked out is taken seriously, it could solve a second major problem in medicine—the high cost of medical training. Edelstein and Jackson are third-year med students at Wayne State University in Detroit. They propose that any community in need of a doctor help pay for a medical student's training. In return for this, the student would sign a contract guaranteeing that he would practice medicine in that community for a specified period following his graduation.

Since thousands of promising young men never become doctors because they can't afford the training, and since many communities never find doctors, no matter how much money they spend advertising for them, this plan may be "just what the doctor ordered."

HELP FOR THE UP-AND-OUTER

An attorney once told me, "you'd be amazed at how many of my well-to-do clients can't afford to pick up a luncheon check. Some are not only perpetually broke, but hopelessly in debt."

Occasionally, this private knowledge becomes public embarrassment, when a prominent figure is forced to declare bankruptcy. It happened just the other day. A popular TV star conceded he was hundreds of thousands of dollars in the red, despite many years of phenomenally high earnings.

Such problems are not limited to those whose salaries are in six figures. Management is the name of the money-game, and anyone can overextend himself.

Recognizing that debtors come in all income brackets, some concerned people have begun establishing non-profit organizations to offer free credit-counseling to anyone. They're being formed in many cities. And it's high time the loan-sharks and fast-buck credit consolidators got some reputable competition. Seemingly insurmountable mountains of debt have destroyed careers, marriages, reputations, even lives. Very often, proper counseling can turn those mountains into molehills.

NOTHING "GOOD" OR "BAD" IN ITSELF

For five years, police in Rome have been trying to break up a stolen car operation going on in the city's underground tunnels . . . that seemingly endless maze called The Catacombs.

And for five years, the police have been notably unsuccessful. One officer says the Catacombs now resemble one big junk yard; that's because thieves hide their stolen cars in the Catacombs just long enough to dismantle them so they can sell the parts. Those tunnels twist and turn for some eight miles. They're very dark. So if thieves hear a policeman approaching, they simply grab their tools and slip further back into another passage of the massive tunnel system.

The use of the Roman Catacombs as headquarters for thieves is a new reminder of the ancient truth that few things in life are intrinsically good or bad. Whether it's money, nuclear energy, or political power, it's how we use it that counts. After all, these same Roman Catacombs once served as sanctuary to the first Christians.

NO IVY ON THESE WALLS

Walter T. Stone runs one of the most unusual colleges in the country. Because it isn't a college in the strictest sense—Stone is superintendent of the California Institute for Men, a minimum security prison at Chino, California. But Stone thinks prisons are for training and adjustment—not punishment—so the emphasis at his prison is on education and rehabilitation.

Working on the theory that most of his men are there

118

because they couldn't compete on the outside, Stone is determined to give them the training they need.

And what do they study? Deep sea diving, for one thing, or, there's a course in animal training. Why these unusual skills? Precisely because they are unusual. Divers are in great demand—short supply. And a good diver can make a lot more money than the average hold-up man, with considerably less risk. With more and more zoos and animal parks springing up around the country, trained handlers can easily get jobs. It must be working, four inmates asked for—and got—permission to stay in prison beyond their terms, just so they could complete their courses.

TO EDIT OR NOT TO EDIT!!

The topic: profanity . . . and when it should, or should not, be permitted on the air. All of the mass media have undergone changes in their approach to censorship, and the American screen has reached a point where practically anything goes. Radio and television, too, have loosened up considerably in their approach to presenting life as it is, although many of the old taboos remain.

A good case certainly can be made for retaining certain word restrictions in entertainment shows presented during hours when children and young people are apt to be tuned in. But should the same, strict standards of speech and conduct apply to news broadcasts? For instance, if a speaker at a public event uses foul language in attacking the President, or for that matter, simply trying to stir up the emotions of the crowd, is it good, honest journalism, to delete those remarks? FCC Chairman Dean Burch thinks not. He says it's probably a little prudish to clean up for the air profanity which was

119

heard by thousands at a news event. And we think he's probably right.

SO YOU WANT SOME GOOD NEWS

People often say to me, "Why don't you newsmen ever report good news?" The truth is we do—more often than people notice—but maybe we need to call more attention to it. So, brace yourself: Here is some good news. It's a set of statistics from the latest United States census which shows illiteracy in this country was cut in half during the decade of the 60's. Considering that just about every other problem increased during that period—crime—inflation—pollution—it's comforting to know that at least one of society's illnesses is responding to treatment.

Ten year ago, more than 2½-million Americans over the age of fourteen were unable to read or write. Now the figure is *under* 1½-million; this, despite the fact that the number of people over fourteen has increased by nearly 22 million. The decline in illiteracy has occurred among both blacks and whites, with blacks, seemingly, benefiting most. According to the census figures, 99 out of 100 Americans over fourteen can now read and write.

Since we're constantly kicking ourselves for what we haven't done, maybe this one little pat on the back won't spoil us.

EVEN THE MARINES ARE CHANGING

From the halls of the Pentagon to the parade grounds of Parris Island the United States Marine Corps is changing. They don't like to talk about it, much. In fact, several high-ranking Marine officers have gone to great pains, explaining that the Marines have no intention of relaxing standards the way the Army, Navy, and Air Force have done.

But for all their tough talk, the Corps is becoming softer in style, if not in substance. True, the leathernecks haven't tried to turn their barracks into Ivy League dormitories, the way the Army has. But any brand-new boot-camp recruit can notice significant changes in the Marine Corps, from the moment he steps off the bus at the basic training depot.

Not so long ago, the new recruit was met with fearsome shrieks of . . . "Move it, you idiots!" . . . "all right you miserable so-and-so's . . ." Now, he's greeted by a sergeant who *smiles,* and in an almost gentle voice explains, "Gentlemen, the first thing you will learn is the position of attention." Does that sound like material for a John Wayne movie?

SOMEDAY

Someday, man will learn to fly. Oh, you thought that challenge was met when the Wright brothers sputtered off the ground at Kitty Hawk? Wrong. That was a technological break-through, all right, but that was an *airplane* flying—not *man.*

Man hasn't given up his age-old dream of breaking gravity's grip, without the aid of a combustion engine, a jet, or a rocket. In fact, Jonathan Mead, a Tufts University graduate student, has won a $1000 Engineering prize for building a scale model of a plane which he claims will enable a man to pedal his way into the sky.

To build the full-scale, flying version of the plane, Mead figures he'll need about $12,000. But, thanks to space-age technology, with its lighter and stronger materials, Mead is convinced that a 140-lb. pilot can get his motorless plane airborne—and keep it up—with no more effort than peddling a hundred-pound bicycle up a ten percent grade. After a couple of years refining his design, Mead hopes to enter a British competition that's offering $24,000 for a successful fly-it-yourself demonstration. Oh yes . . . Mead calls his 18-mile-an-hour plane the SST—Super-Slow Transport.

IT'S SUCH A COMFORT

It could turn out to be the tortoise-and-the hare story of the century . . . that race between those sleek, 600-mile-an-hour jetliners and those slow, unglamorous, old oil-burners called—buses. Believe it or not, the buses are ahead, at least where it counts—in the pocketbook.

America's twelve major airlines report *losses* last year of $123,000,000. But the nation's biggest transcontinental busline shows a $32,000,000 *profit*.

There are many reasons for the bus-business boom. The most obvious is cost. A round-trip from New York to Washington, for instance, is $35 cheaper by bus than by plane. And, on such short trips, the bus can be almost as fast—considering the time it takes to drive to and from the airport, plus time lost idling on the runway or circling, due to high-density air traffic. But another big reason folks are finding it such a comfort to take the bus is precisely that—comfort. Today's air-conditioned, snack-serving, hostess-equipped vehicle with its built-in rest-room and piped-in music is a far cry from the depressing and smelly old clunker they used to call a bus.

ART COVERS A MULTITUDE OF SINS

Frank Perry of Fort Myers, Florida, doesn't really consider himself an artist. But having seen some of the stuff being successfully passed off as art in various contests, Frank decided to give it a try. His very first painting won fourth place in a show sponsored by the Art Council of Southwest Florida. The judges may have been a bit perturbed when Frank divulged that he'd created the masterpiece by covering a canvas with violet and grey paint—then backing the left wheel of his car over it.

And if that doesn't suggest that the word "art" today covers a multitude of sins, then how about the abstraction Michael Heizer is hoping to produce on the lawn of the Detroit Institute of Arts? Heizer wants to drag a 35-ton slab of granite across the fresh sod, the lawn they spent four thousand dollars to install. Heizer says if they'll let him scoop out several ruts in the lawn, he'll call the finished sculpture—"Earthworks." It may sound like the insensitive observation of an uncultured slob—but may I suggest that *if* the Detroit Institute approves Heizer's art-work, more than the lawn is going to get gouged.

JUST NOT MY BAG

Today's item is a warning to men everywhere about the newest thing in male fashions. And I don't think you're going to like it—pocketbooks. I mean over-the-shoulder bags—purses for men—*just like the ladies* have worn or carried for years!

Call it a fad, if you want to, the fact is, the fashion experts are dead serious about it. Already a lot of businessmen in big cities such as New York and Los Angeles are carrying the men's shoulder bags. And they use them just about the way their wives do—for credit cards—wallet—comb—keys—handkerchief—cough drops—sun glasses—note-pad; one guy even carries a bottle of after-shave in his purse.

With the bags selling from $50 to $120, it's easy

to see why the fashion industry is pushing the idea. Well, for my money, they can just keep pushing. I can dig the wide ties, wide lapels, fitted suits—even mod hair styles, but me carry a purse? Sorry, Madison Avenue, that's just not my bag.

CARRIED TO A CONCLUSION

Today's comment is entitled, "Women's Liberation" . . . subtitled . . . "Where will it all end?"

Maybe you saw that newspaper article announcing that the Louisville Area Council on Religion and Race has dropped the term, chairman. From now on, it's chair*person*. According to the article, this could become the starting signal for a complete purge of our chauvinistic language. Maybe all terms which include the masculine form should be rid of such bias by substituting a neutral word. For instance, factory supervisors would no longer be foremen, they'd become fore*persons*. Congress, of course, could refer to its members as Congress-*persons*. Clergymen would become clergy*persons* . . . night-watchmen, night-watch-*persons*. The possibilities boggle the mind. Consider the new Navy, with its new uniforms and relaxed code of conduct. Surely the Navy will want to toss overboard that archaic term, seaman, in favor of sea*person*. Why, even the slang expression, *son*-of-a-gun, might be changed to *child*-of-a-gun . . .

And who can say just how much these long-overdue changes would benefit humanity? Pardon me, ladies . . . I meant to say, hu-*person*-ity???

THE HIGH COST OF SAFETY

The problem with trying to make anything absolutely safe is that by the time we've accomplished it, the product—or service—is so costly, no one can afford it.

Each time Detroit adds a safety device to cars, the price goes up.

So, we compromise—and reason usually brings us out somewhere between Ralph Nader, who wants absolute product safety, and industry, which too often seems willing to barter customer protection for bigger profits.

According to dental experts at Columbia University, it's even possible, now, to keep our teeth—for life—and without cavities—*if* we're willing to pay the price. The price, in this case, is a tooth care procedure which involves staining the teeth with food coloring (to make plaque visible), rinsing away excess food stain, inspecting each tooth with a flashlight and mirror, brushing away stained material from each tooth with fluoridated toothpaste, and cleaning between all teeth with dental floss.

That procedure is to be followed **after every meal,** (which shouldn't be too often). I mean, doing all that, who'll have time to eat?

HOW HAPPY ARE THE HANDICAPPED?

Dr. Paul Cameron of the University of Louisville, working with a team of Detroit psychologists, has been studying the physically handicapped, trying to determine whether people who are crippled, or whose bodies are malformed, are *any less happy* than those who are physically normal.

The results of the study are enlightening. First of all, they indicate that there is essentially no difference in the degree of satisfaction, or life enjoyment, experienced by the handicapped and those with no physical impairment. In fact, the statistics show that the non-handicapped contemplated suicide, or attempted it, more often than the crippled and malformed.

The project matched people by age, sex, income, and background. The only difference was in their physical normalcy. Within the same income groups, the degree of frustration with life was essentially the same between the normals and the malformed.

It is significant, I think, that the afflicted judged their lives to be more difficult than the lives of normals, but this judgment did not make them less happy.

They have learned one of life's great lessons: happiness is not the result of avoiding adversity—it is the result of coming to terms with it.

THE PERFECT JOB

How come some guys seem to show up for work, full of vinegar, and ready for action with only four or five hours sleep . . . while the rest of us seem to suffer from tired blood, no matter how much sleep we get? Medical experts have been trying to answer that one for decades but so far, there's no general agreement on why sleeping needs vary so much. Several interesting studies, and a few *significant* ones, have been done in this field. One of the most recent was conducted at the Sleep Laboratory of Boston State Hospital.

This study, detailed in the magazine, MODERN MEDICINE, shows that people who can get along on relatively little sleep—say six hours or less—tend to be outgoing, lively, more adept socially, and, more efficient. On the other hand, those of us who like to spend hours and hours studying the interior of our eyelids, tend to be introverted, inhibited, anxious, and, according to the study, depressed.

126

The researchers see a possible relationship between these negative personality traits and the need for more sleep. I don't know about that. But the next time they're looking for volunteers to study sleeping requirements, I'm willing to give my body to science.